Costa Rica
Hummingbirds

a photographic collection

Kimberli A. Bindschatel & Amber G. Elliott

Published by Turning Leaf Productions, LLC.
Traverse City, Michigan

www.KimberliBindschatel.com

ISBN-13:978-1542496230
ISBN-10:1542496233

Thank you for purchasing this book and supporting an indie author.

Costa Rica.
The most biologically diverse place on Earth.
Fifty-four species of hummingbirds.

Since I visited with just a backpack and a pair of binoculars in 2010, I couldn't wait to go back with my camera. The wildlife photography opportunities are unending. In December of 2016, that dream came true when my friend and fellow photographer, Amber Elliott, and I set off on our great Costa Rican adventure. The list of species we had the great experience of seeing is too long to mention. Standing amid a diverse array of hummingbirds flitting all around was surreal. Certainly a once-in-a-lifetime experience.

Pura Vida!

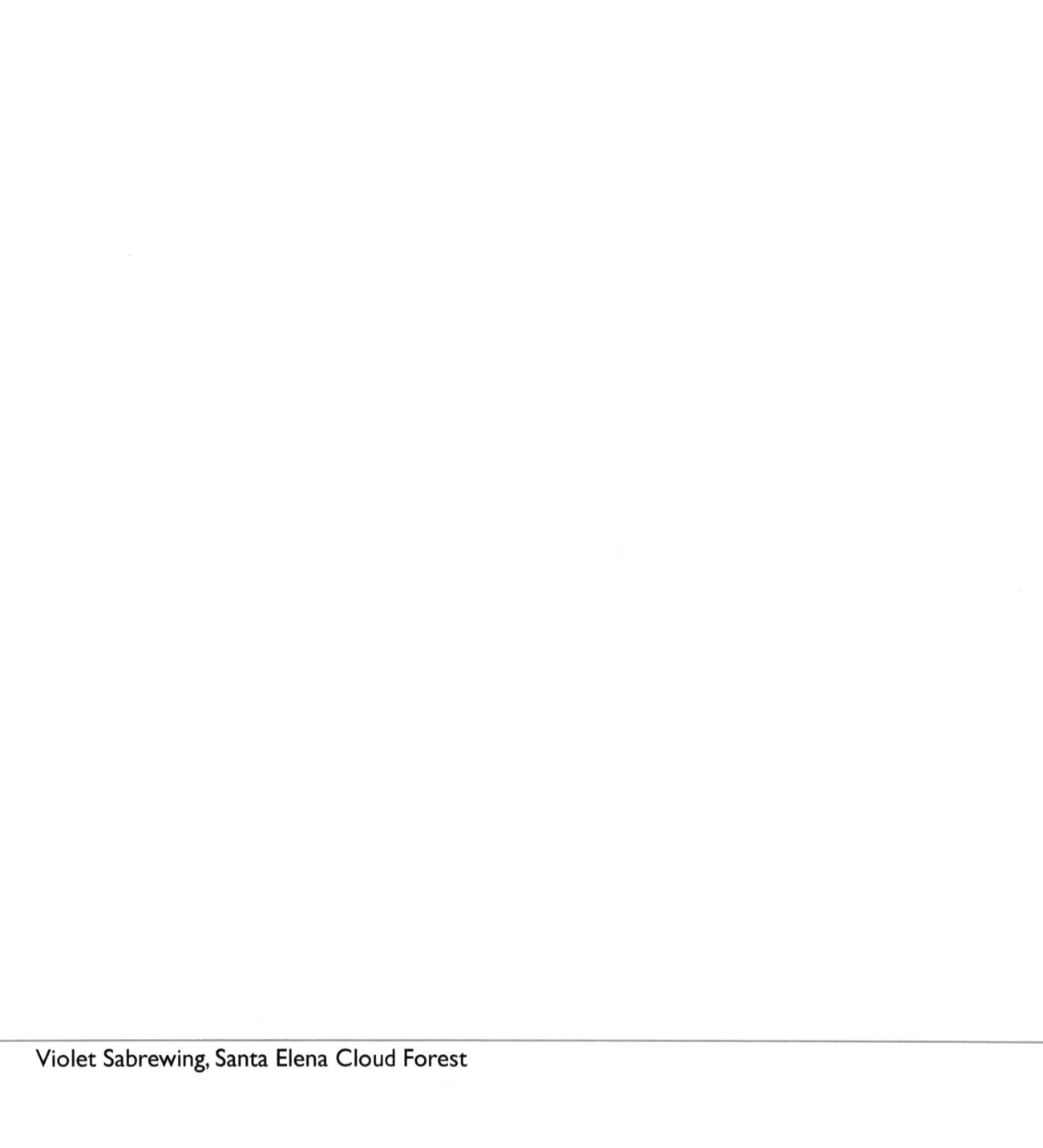

Violet Sabrewing, Santa Elena Cloud Forest

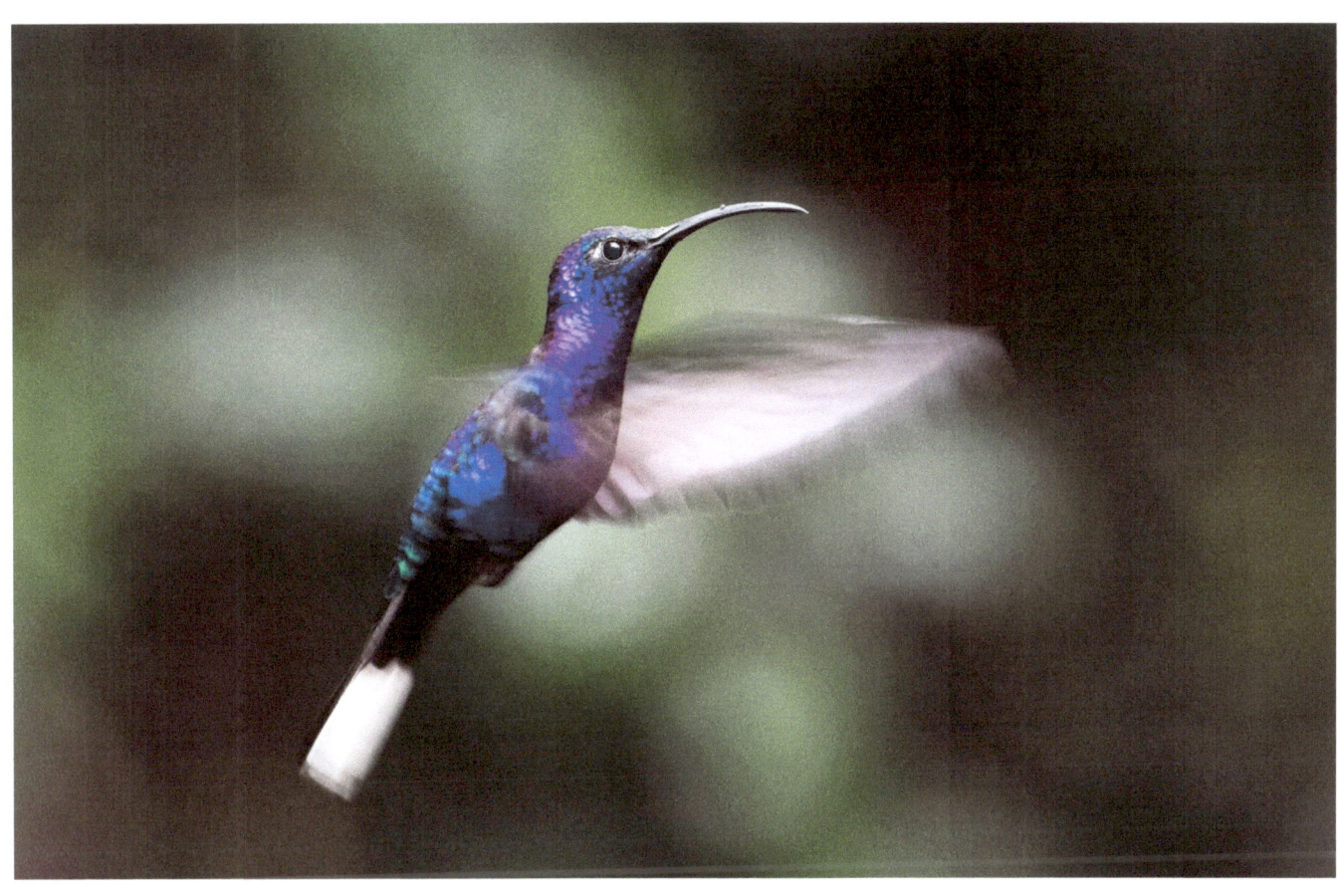

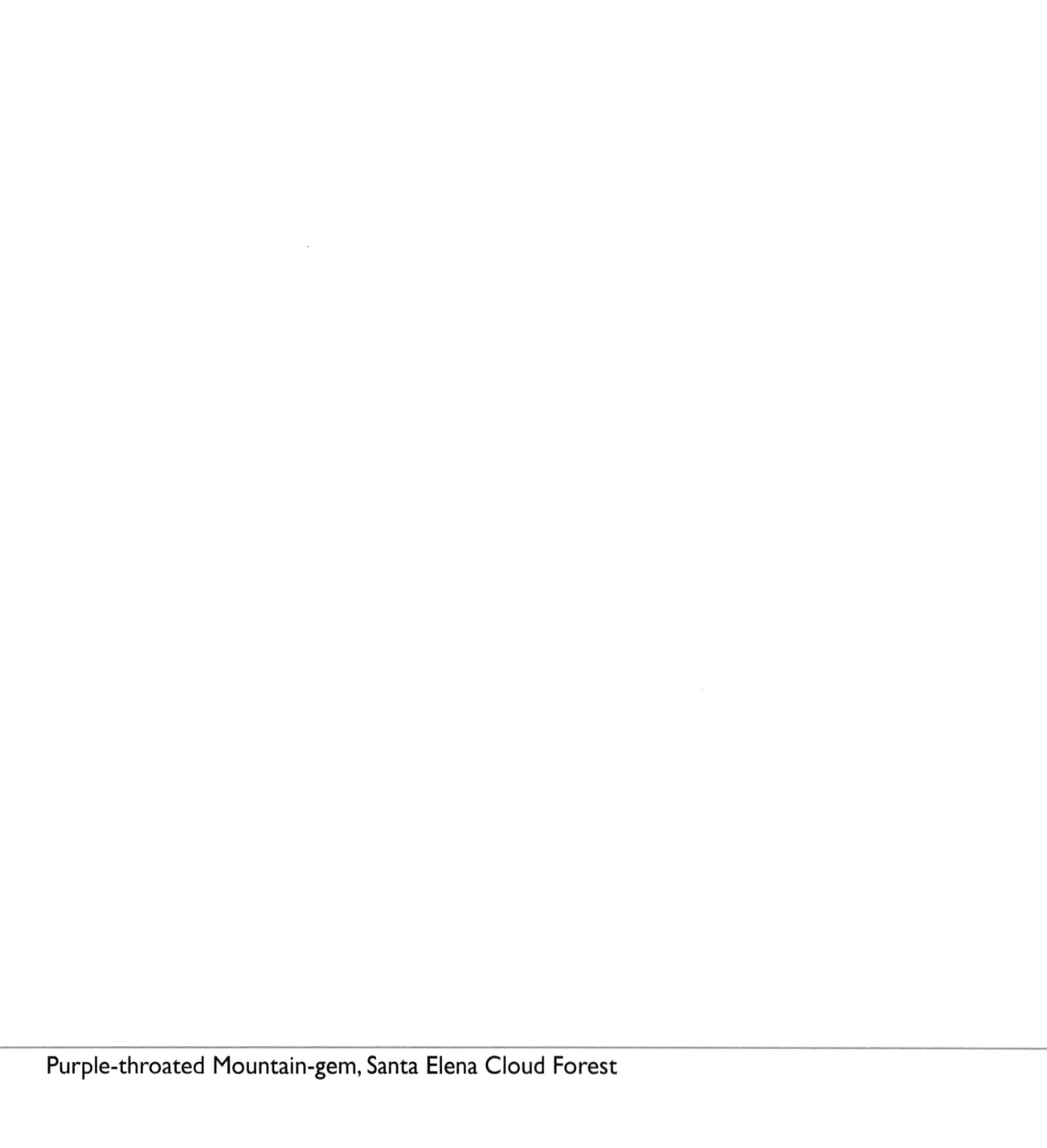

Purple-throated Mountain-gem, Santa Elena Cloud Forest

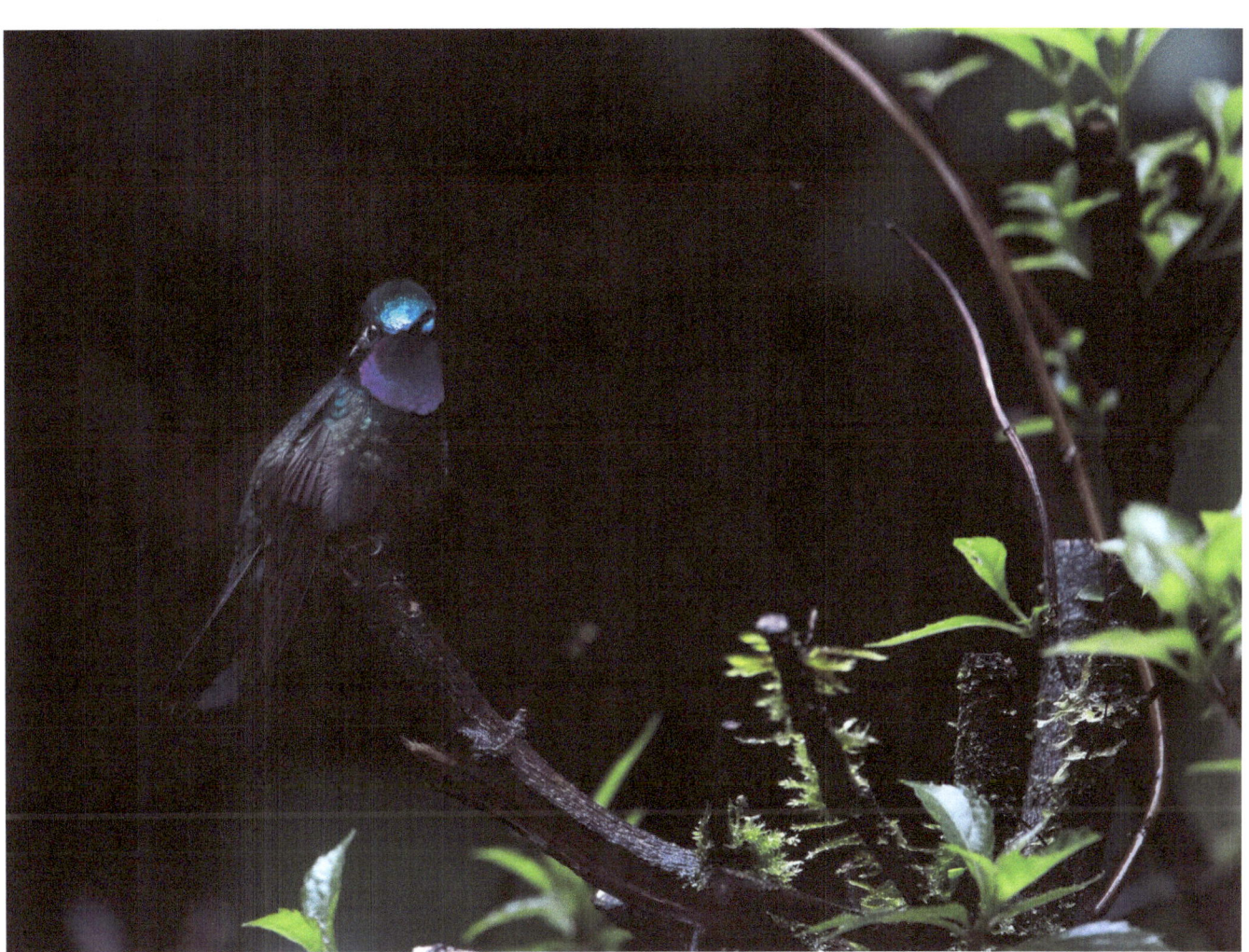

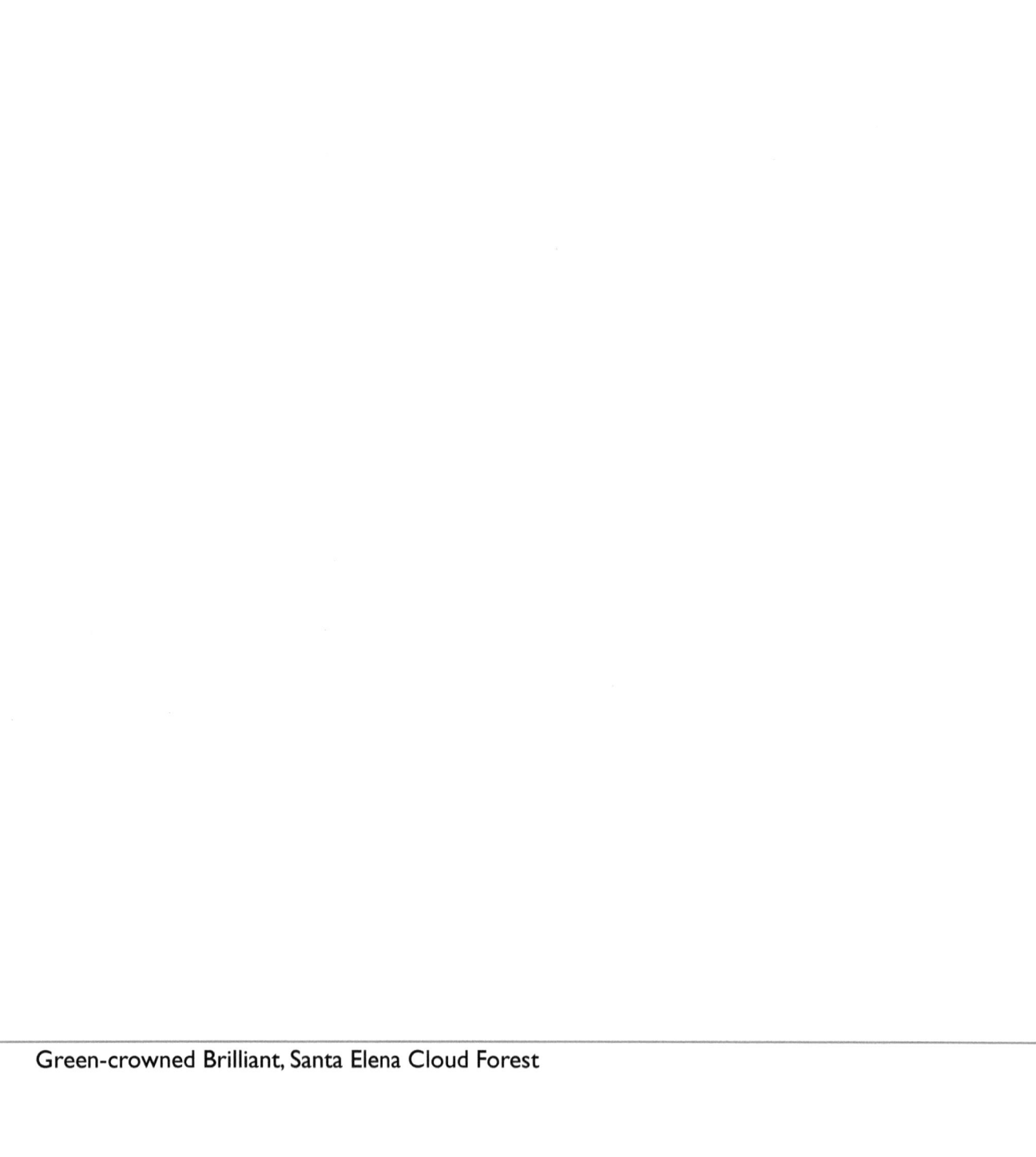

Green-crowned Brilliant, Santa Elena Cloud Forest

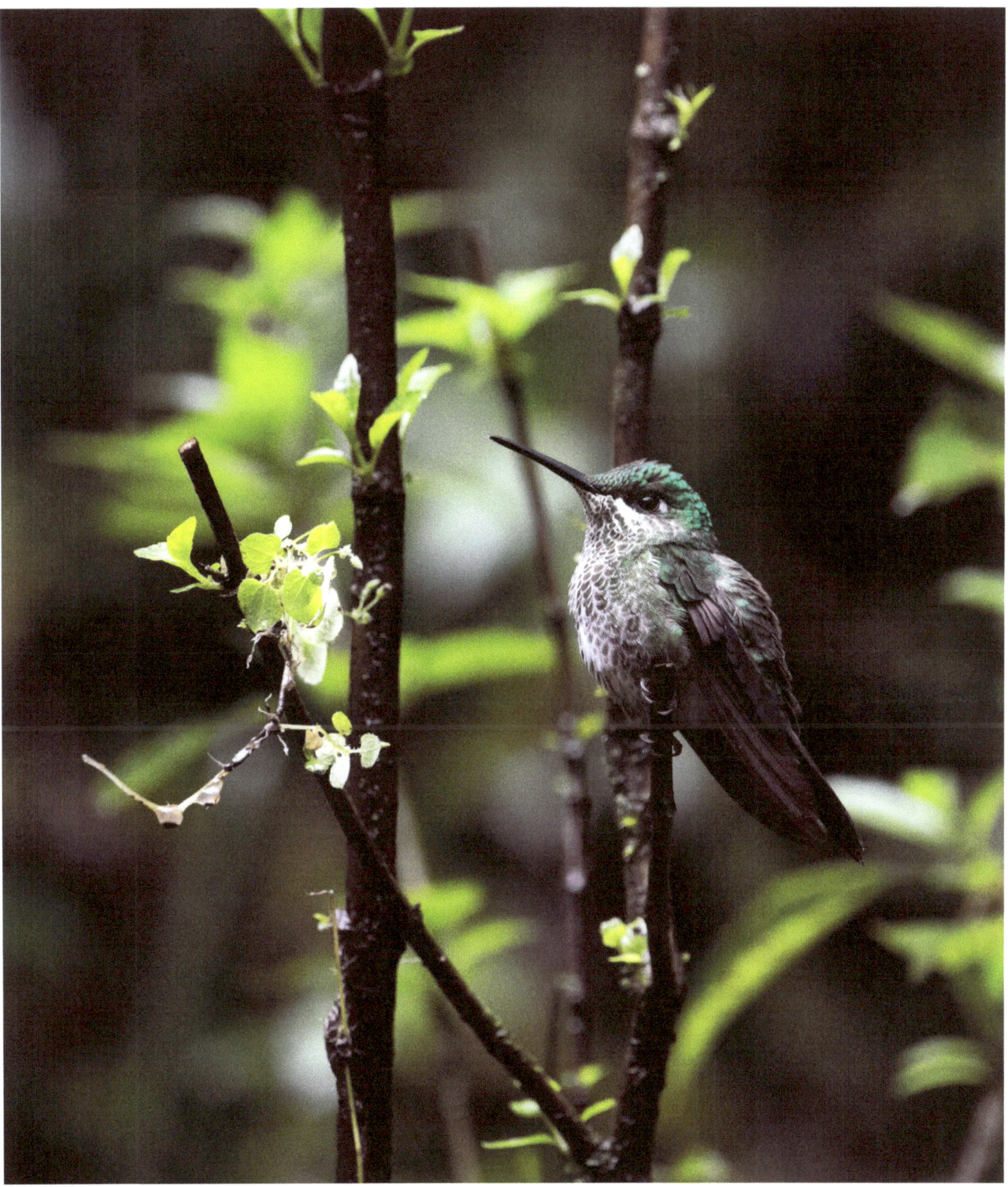

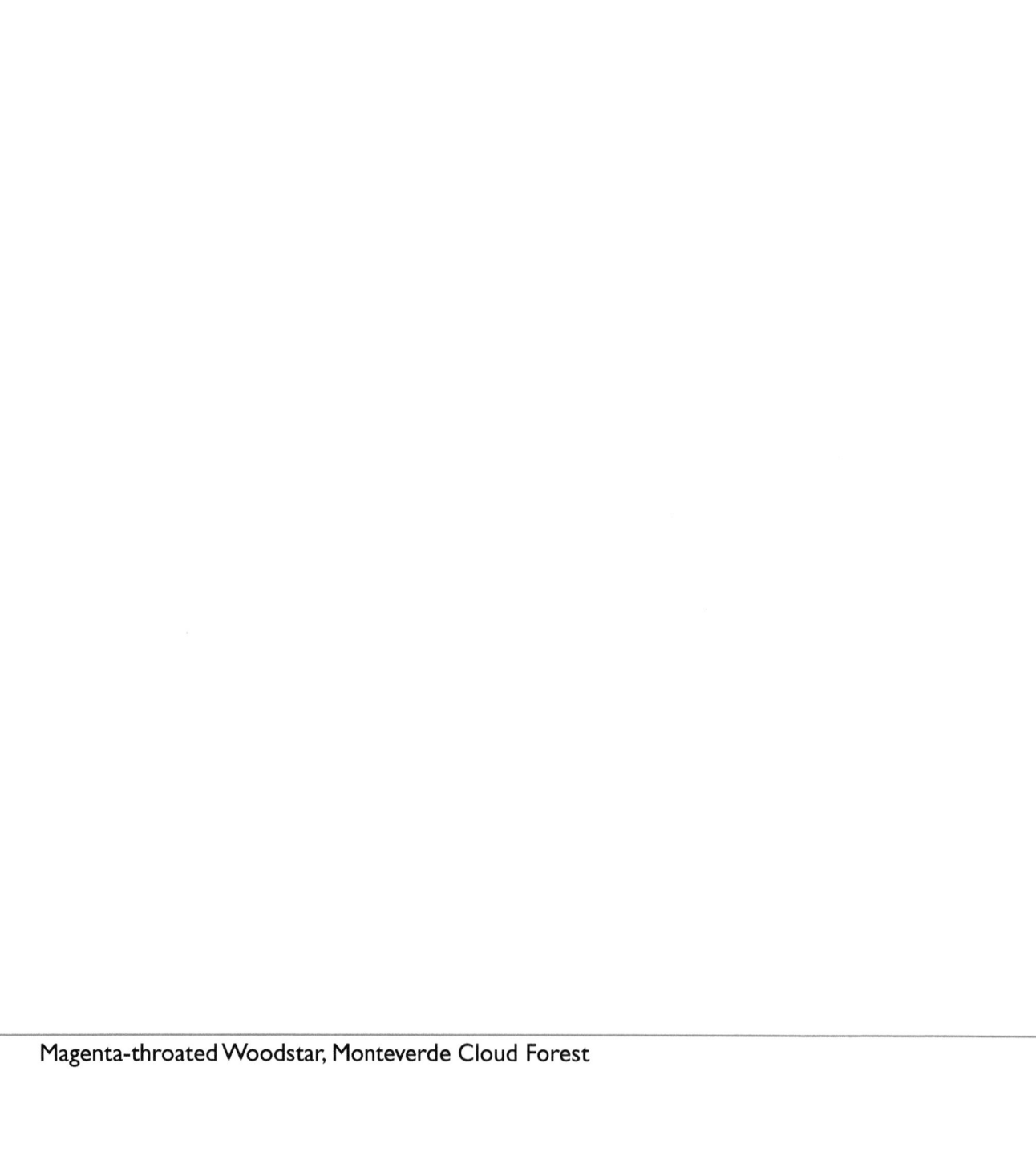

Magenta-throated Woodstar, Monteverde Cloud Forest

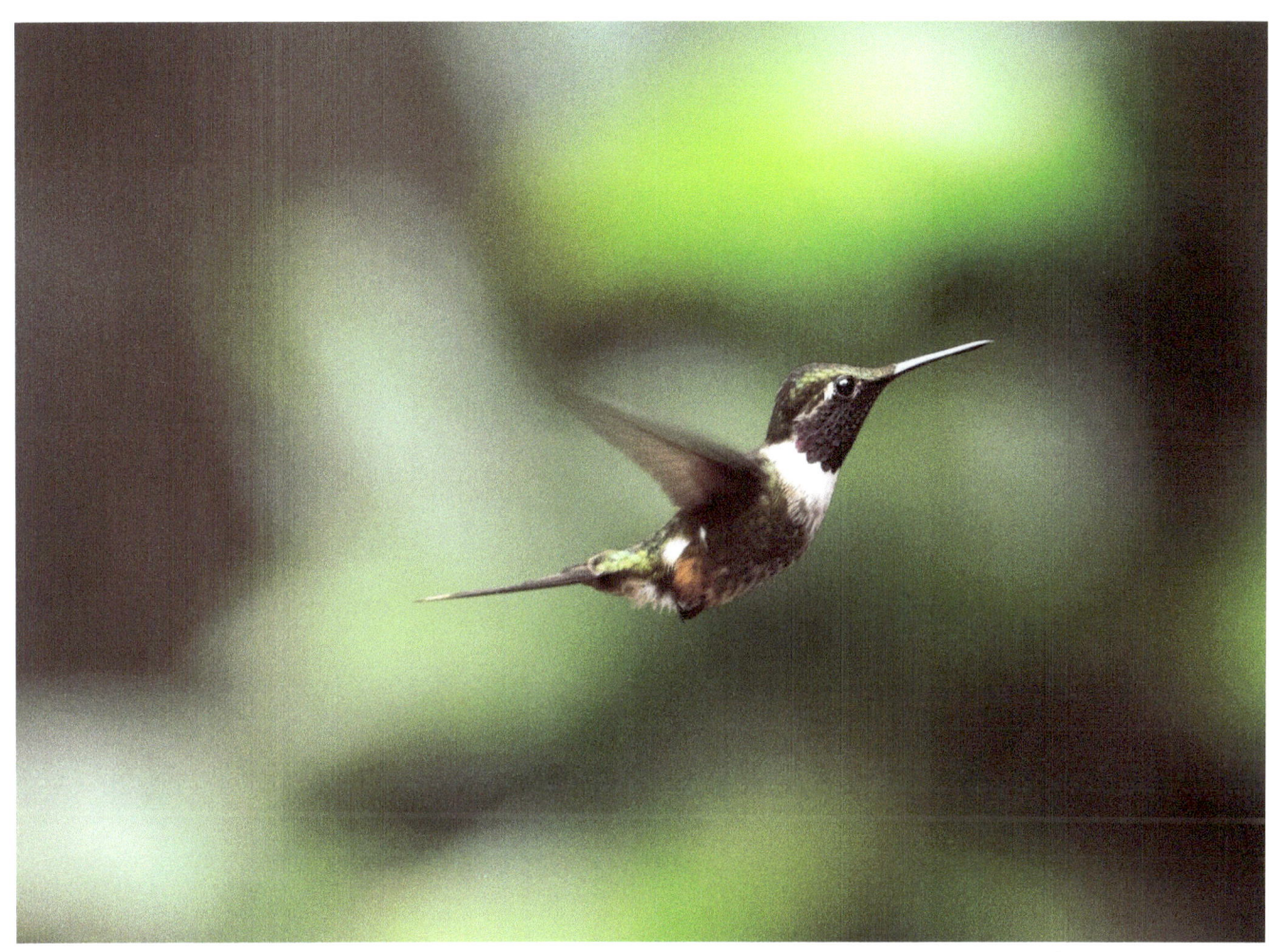

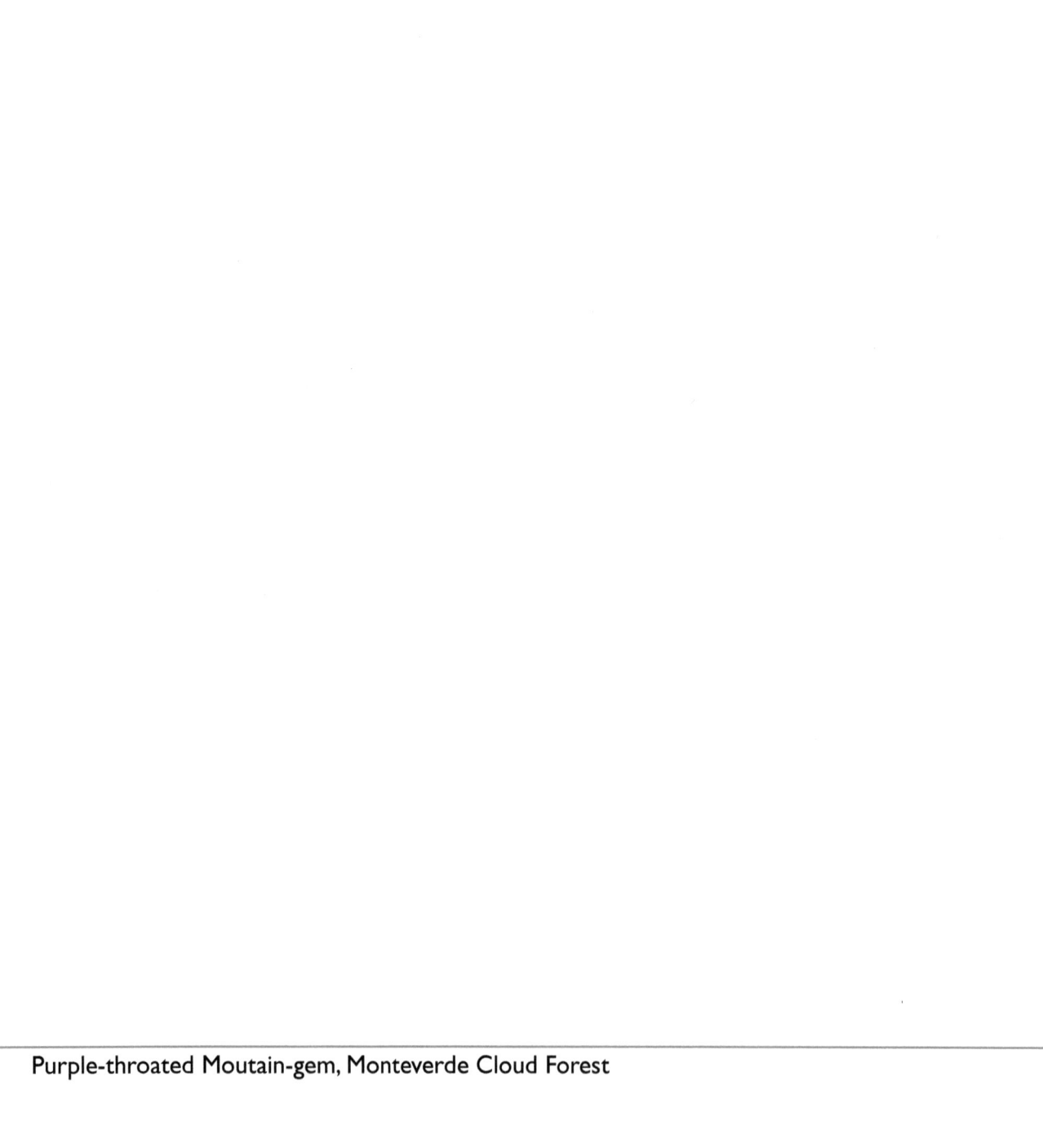

Purple-throated Moutain-gem, Monteverde Cloud Forest

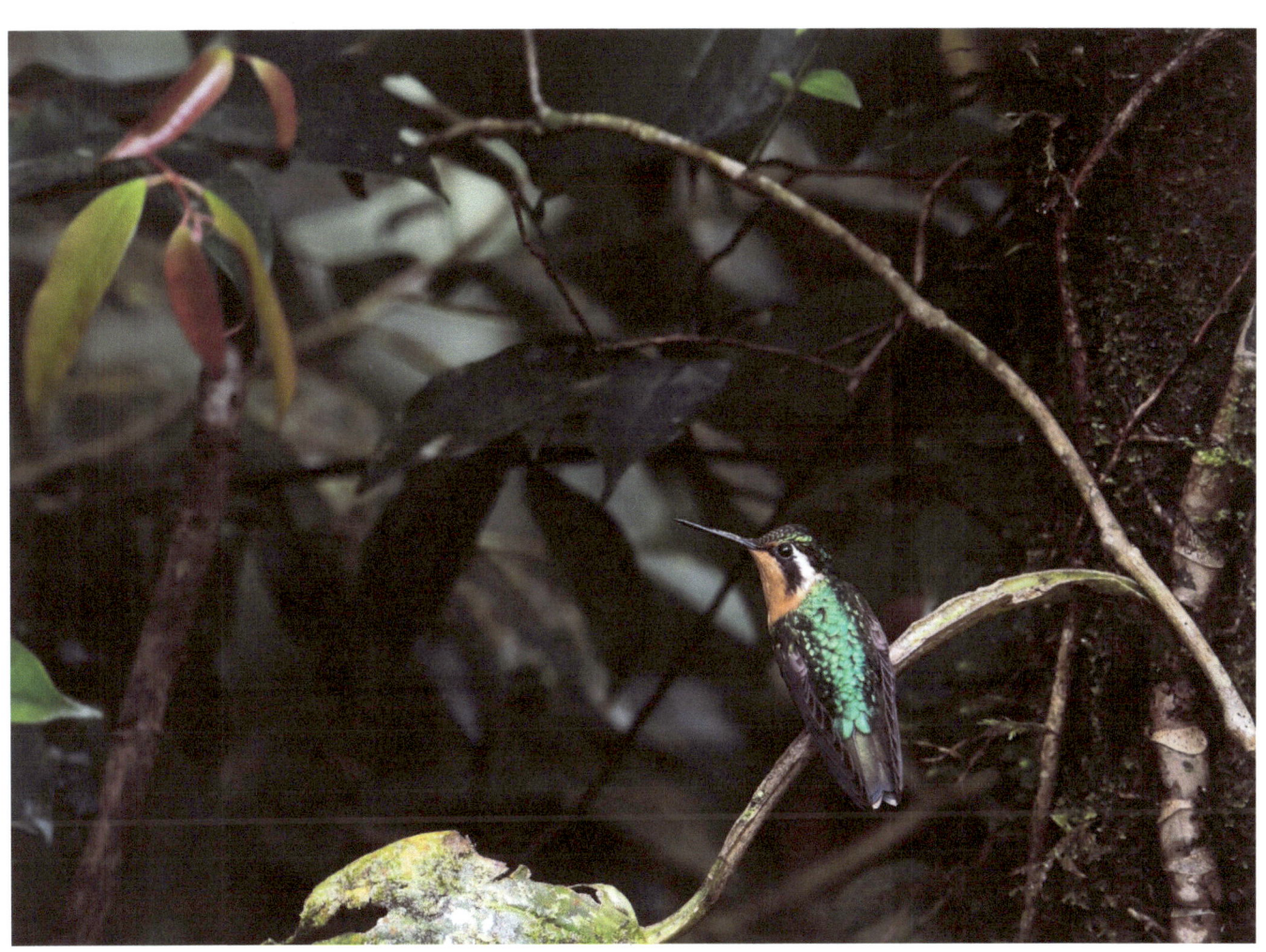

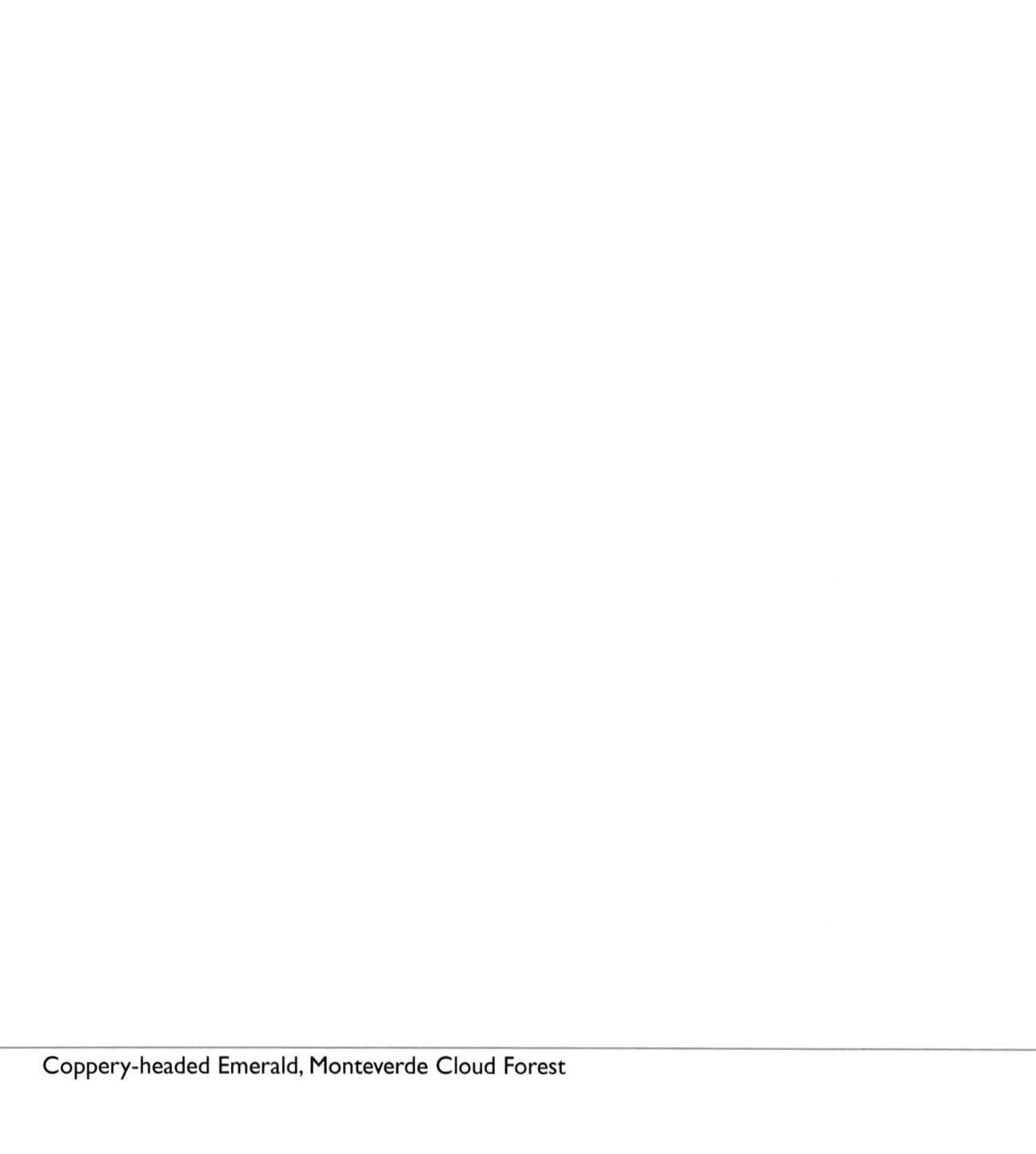

Coppery-headed Emerald, Monteverde Cloud Forest

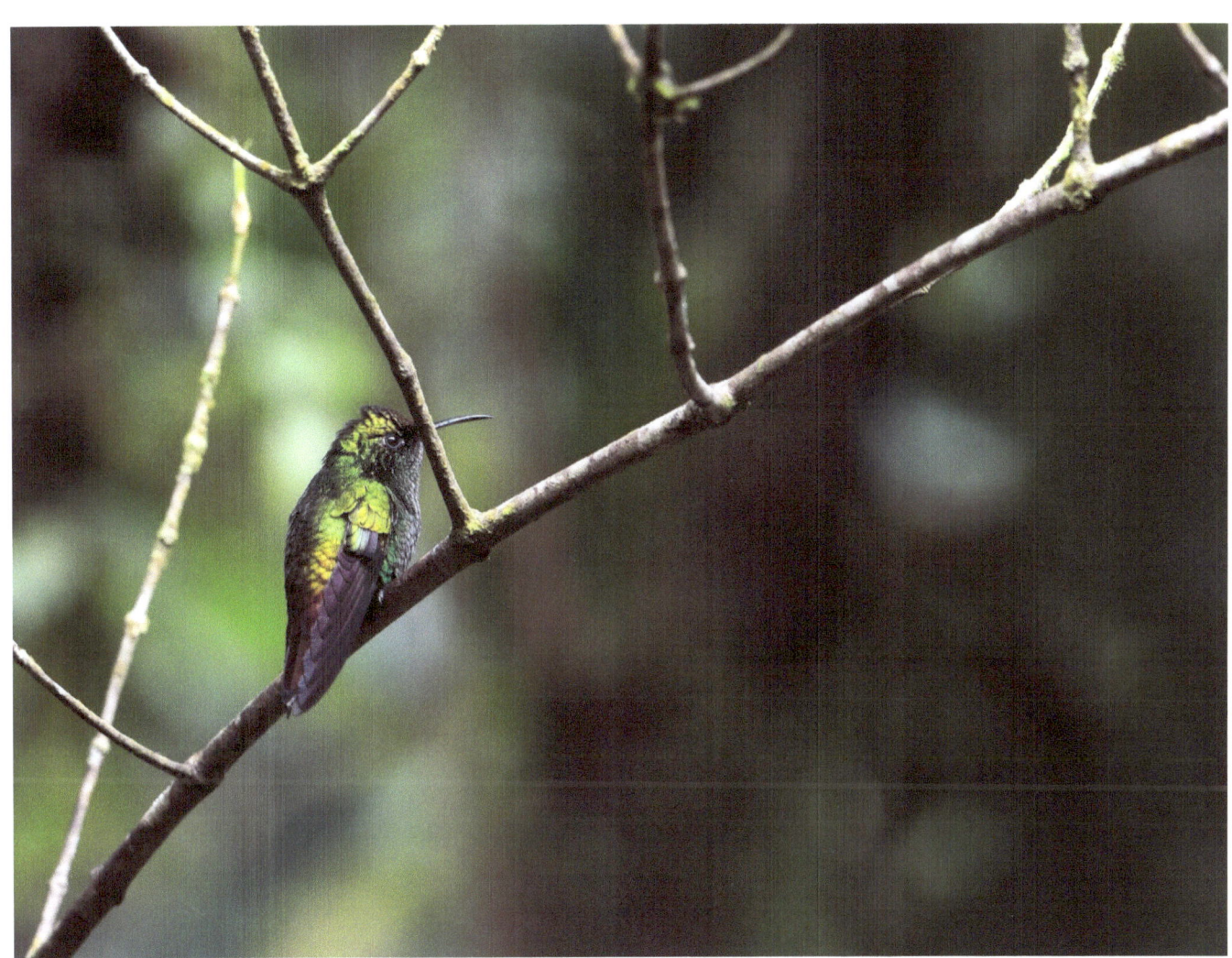

Brown Violet-ear, Monteverde Cloud Forest

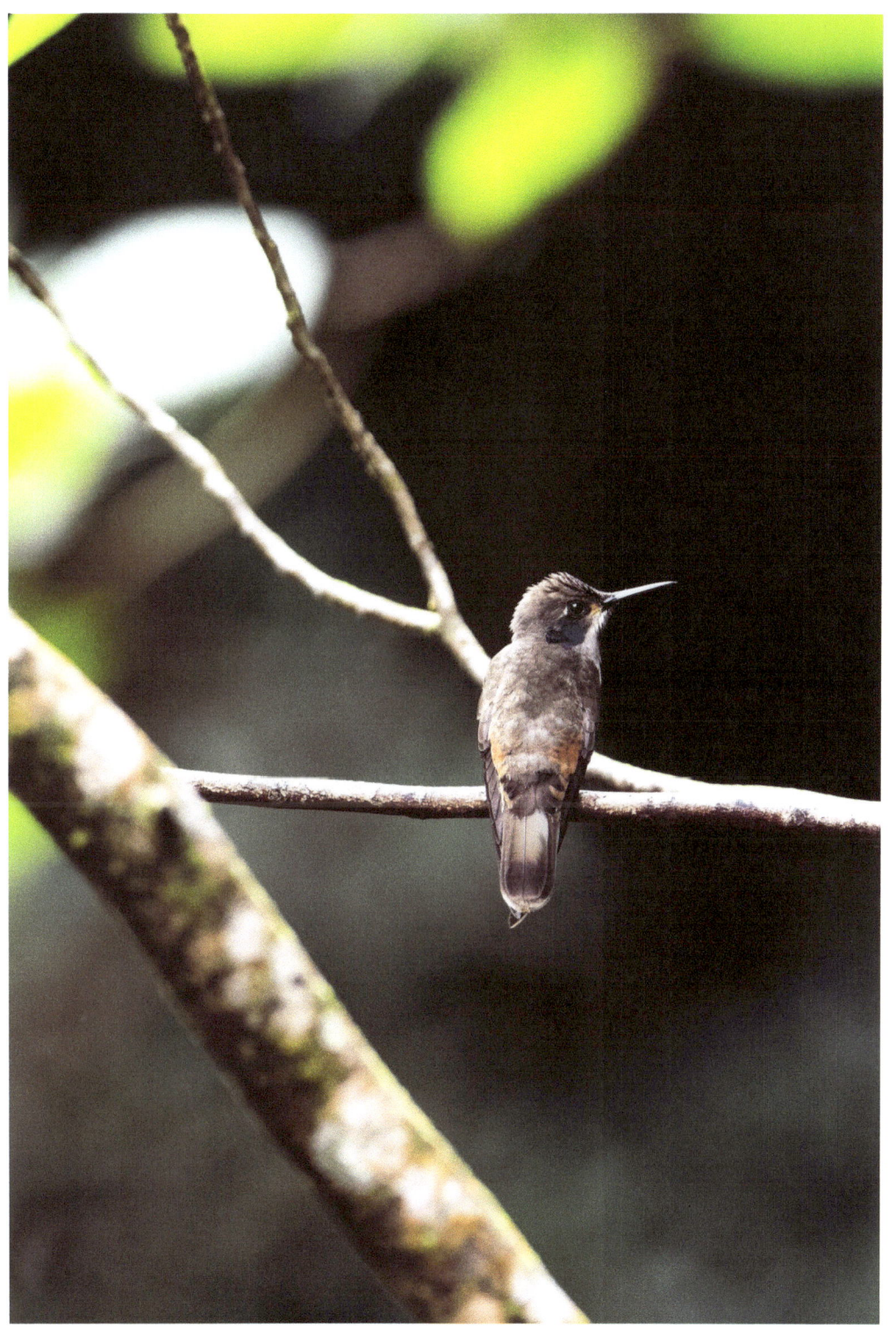

Violet Sabrewing, Monteverde Cloud Forest

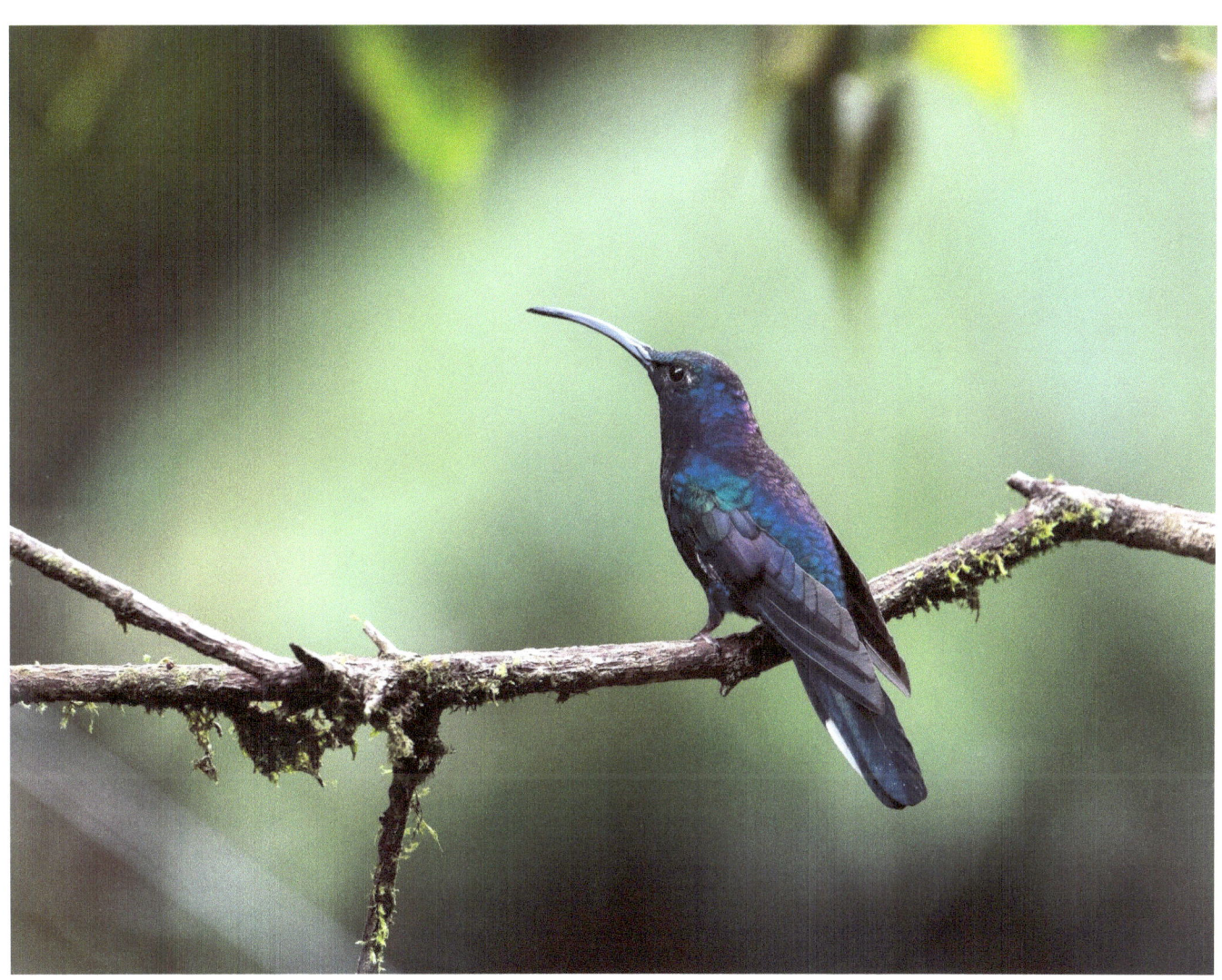

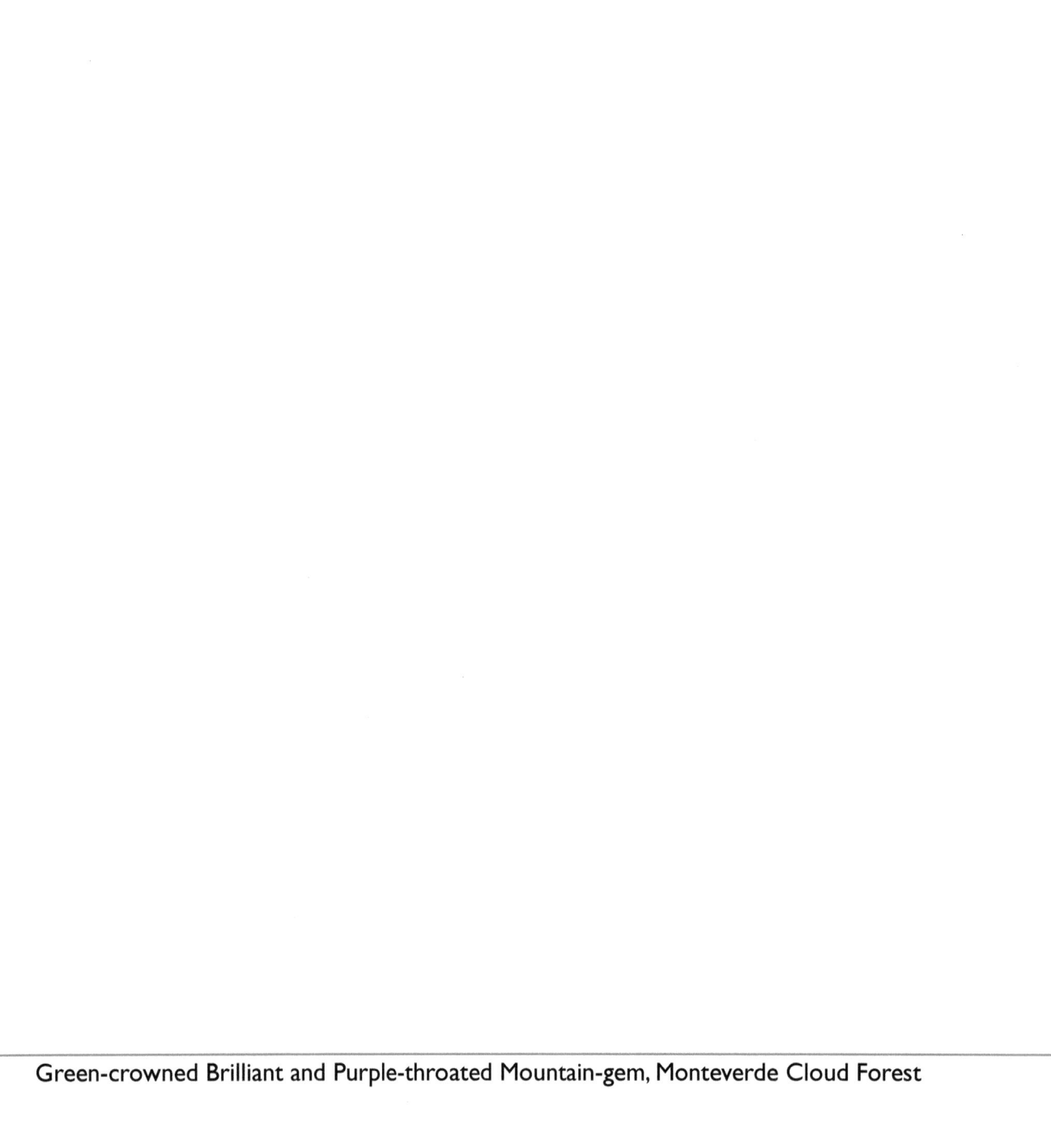

Green-crowned Brilliant and Purple-throated Mountain-gem, Monteverde Cloud Forest

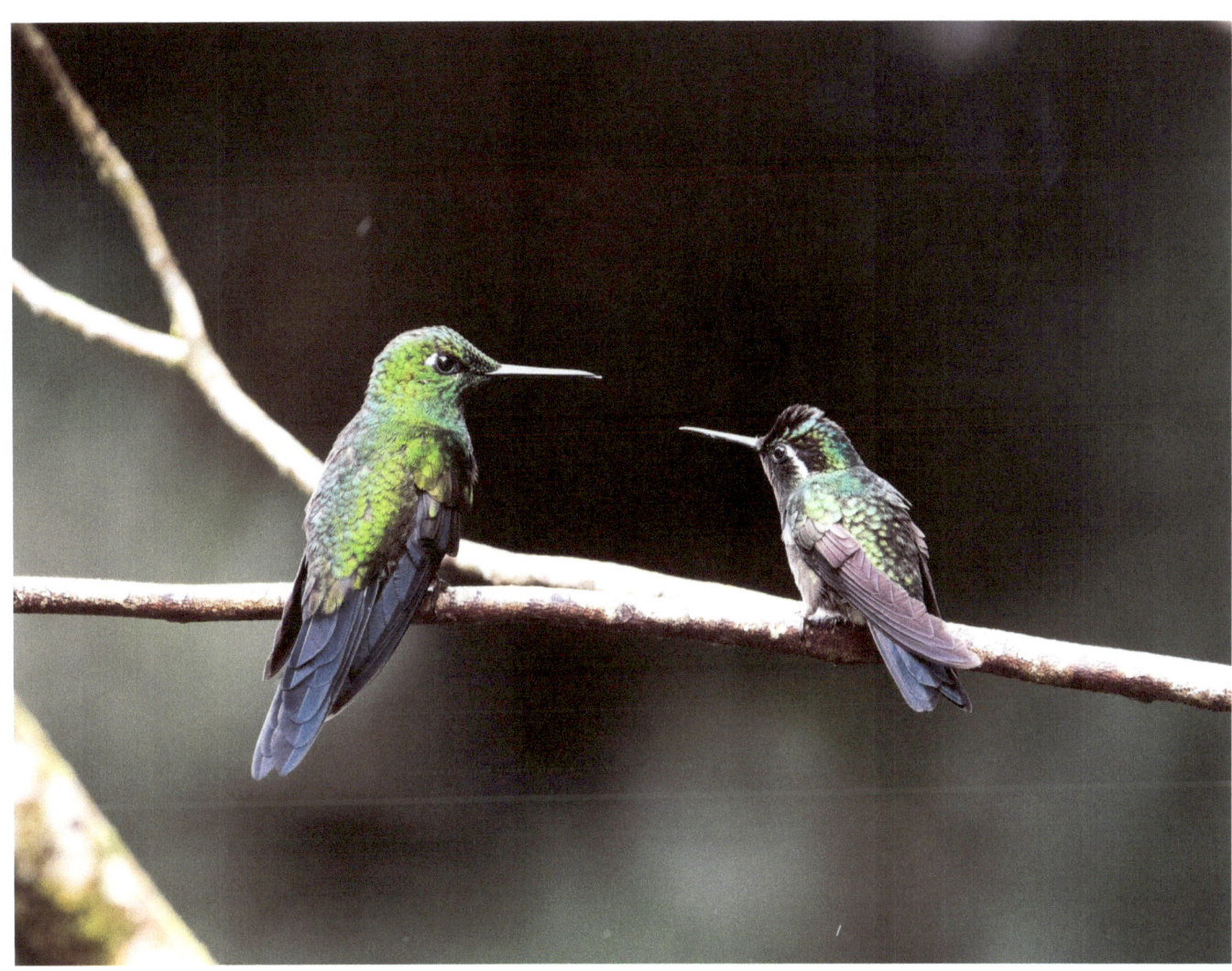

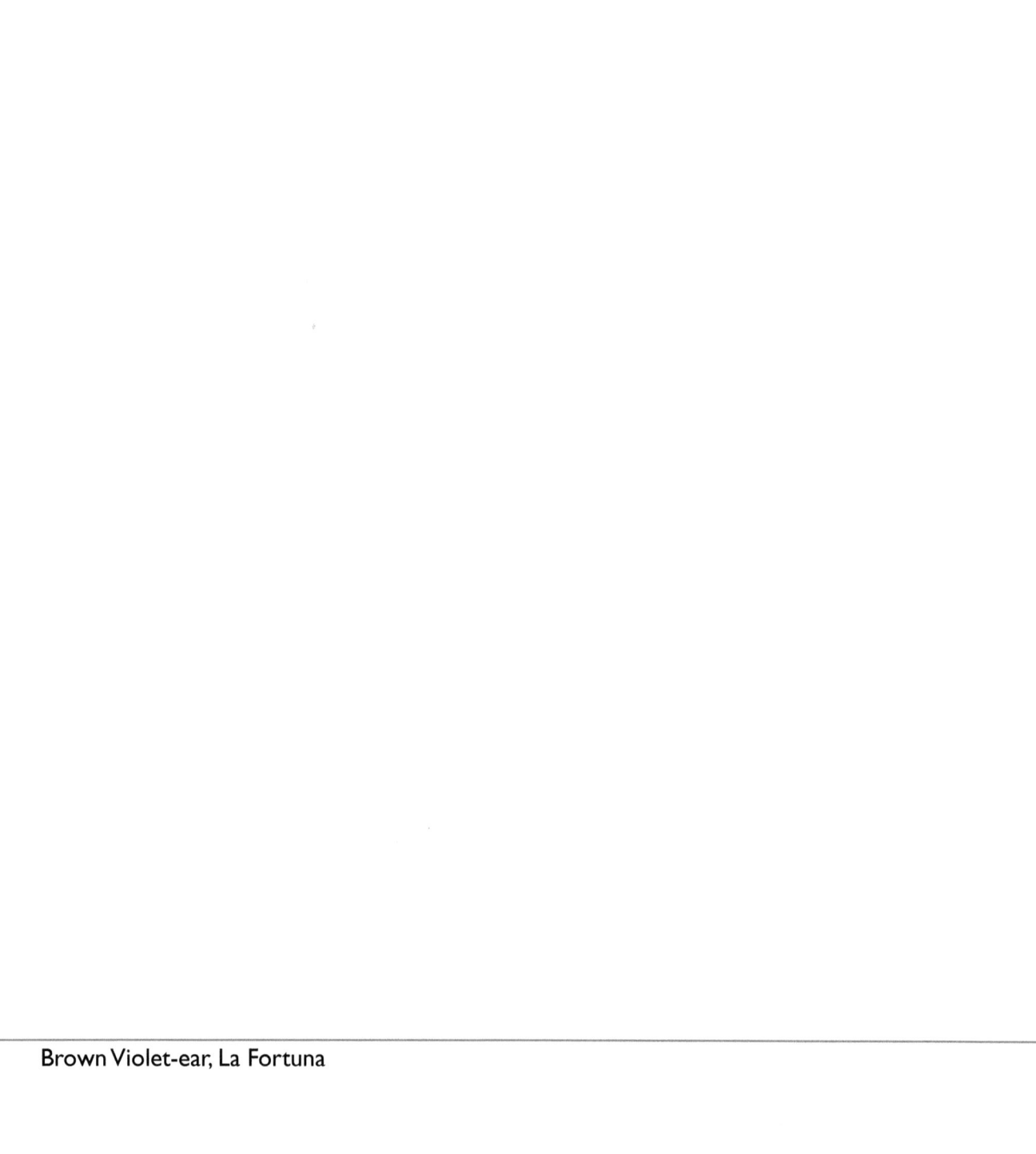

Brown Violet-ear, La Fortuna

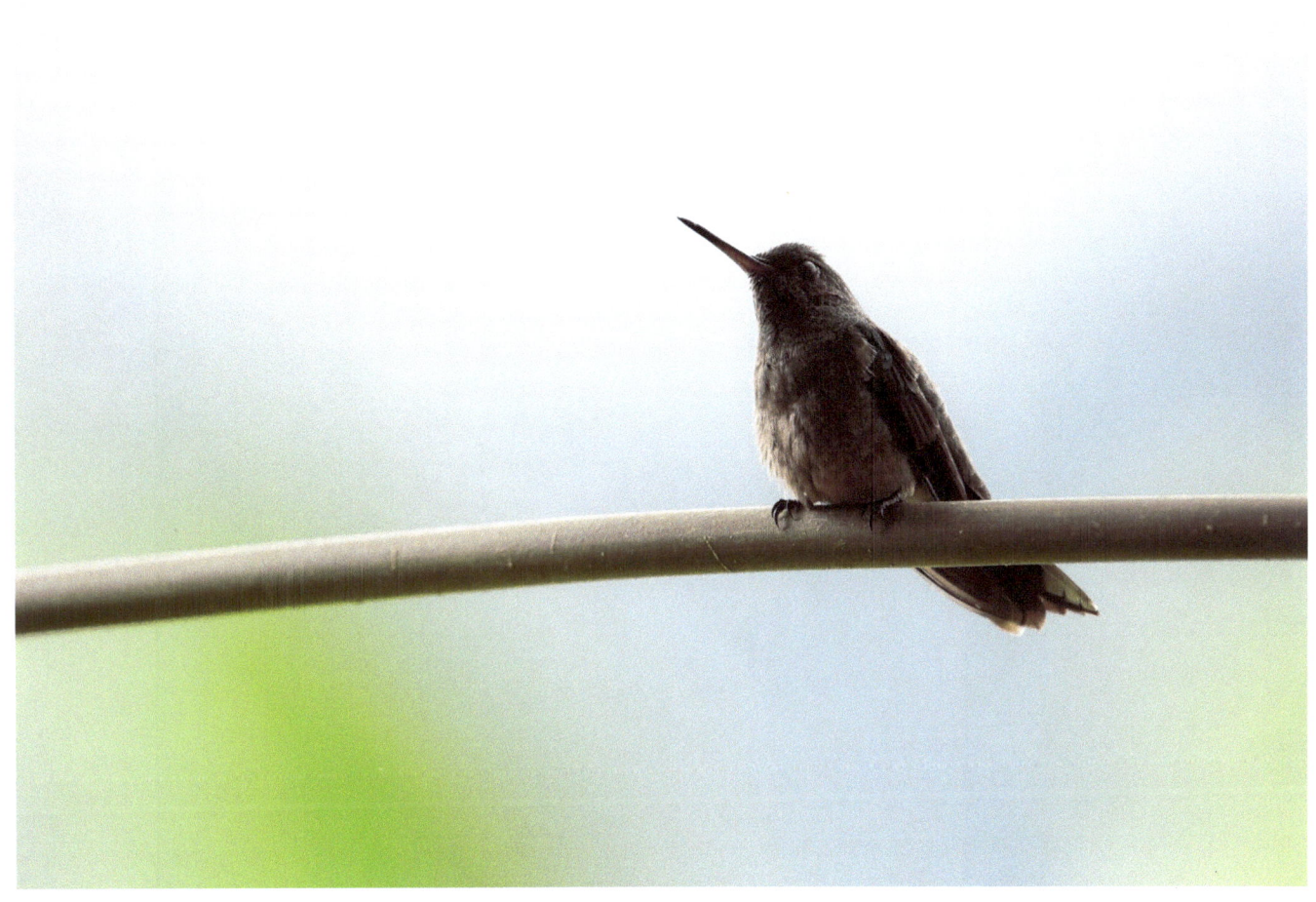

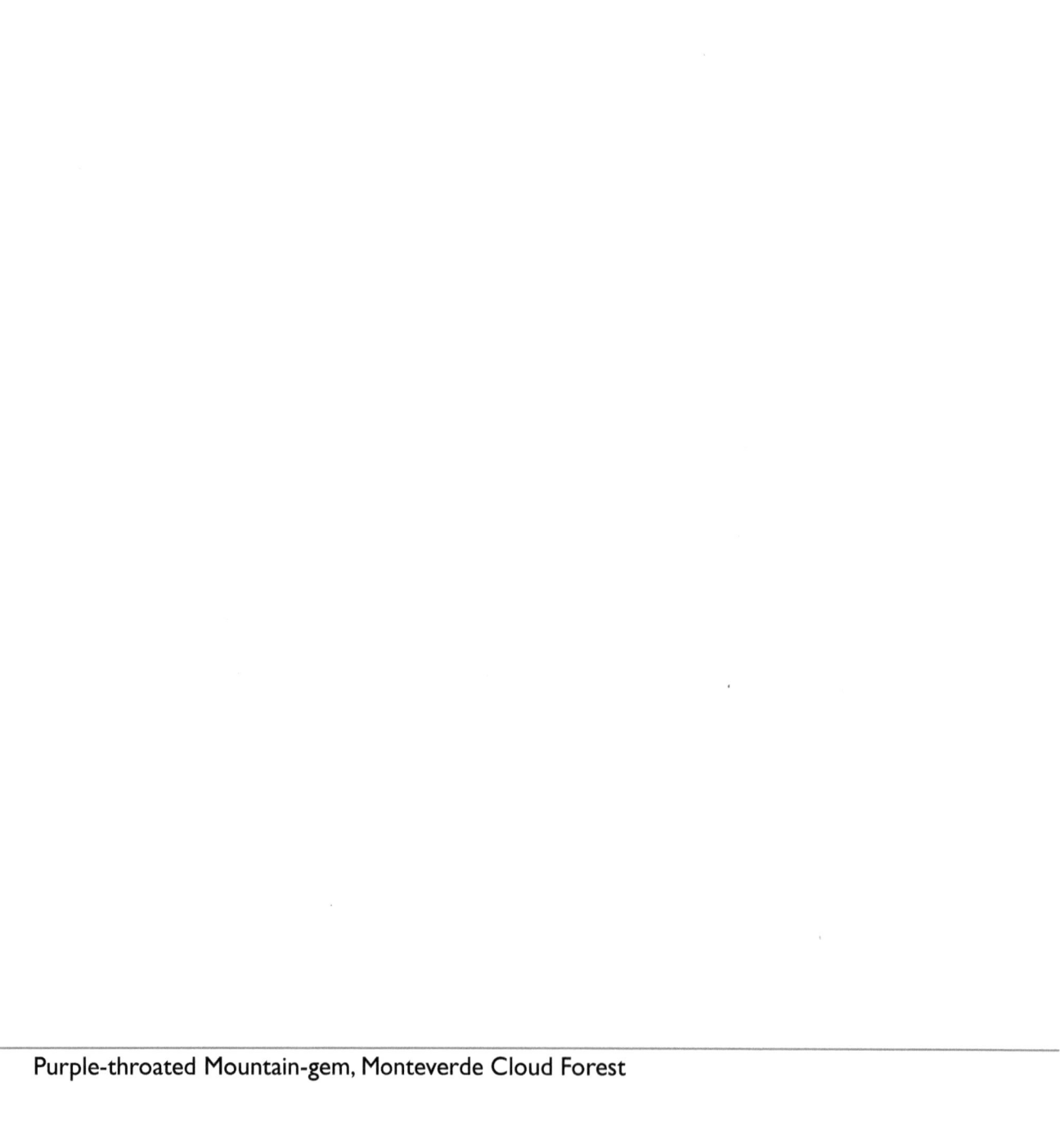

Purple-throated Mountain-gem, Monteverde Cloud Forest

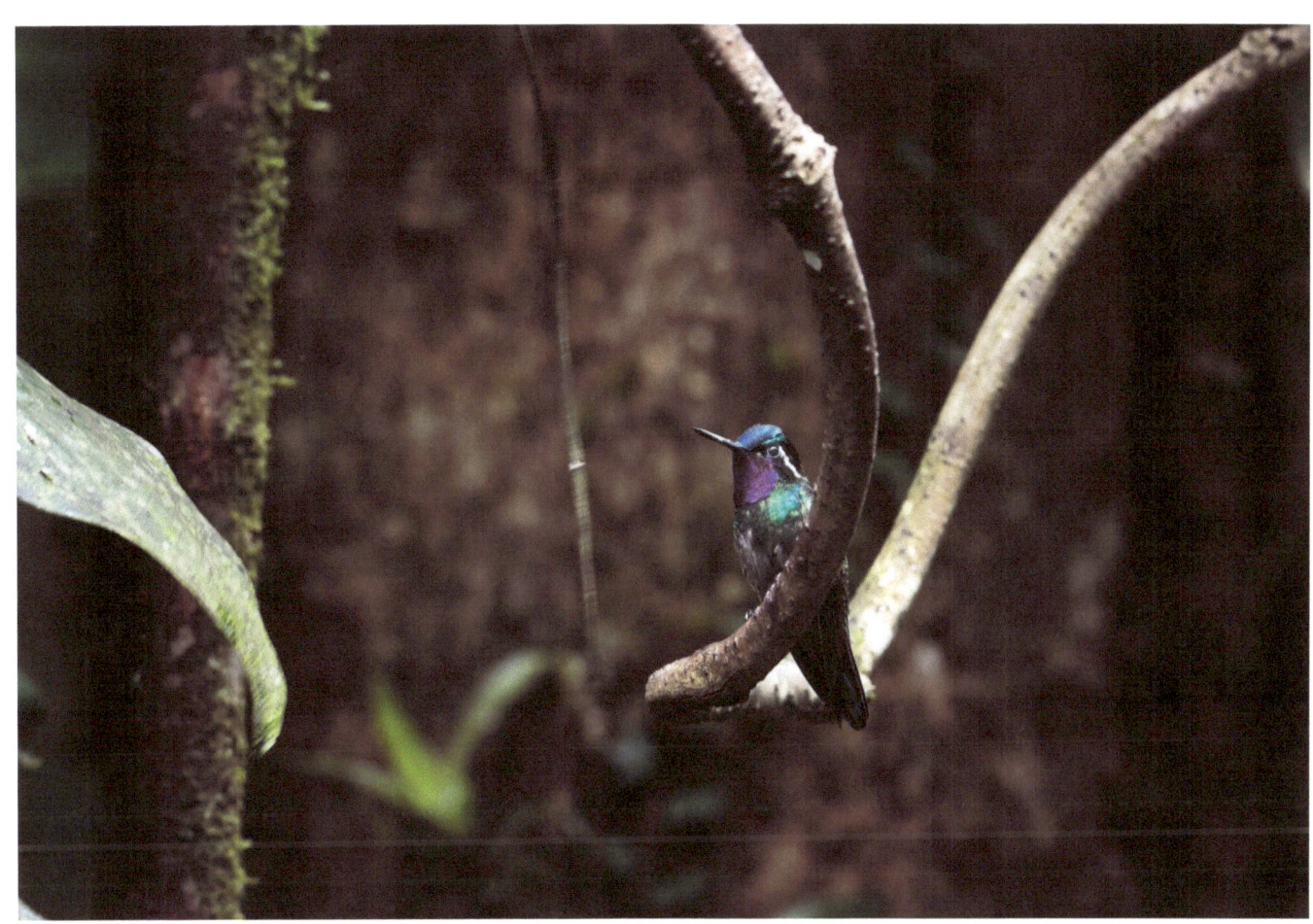

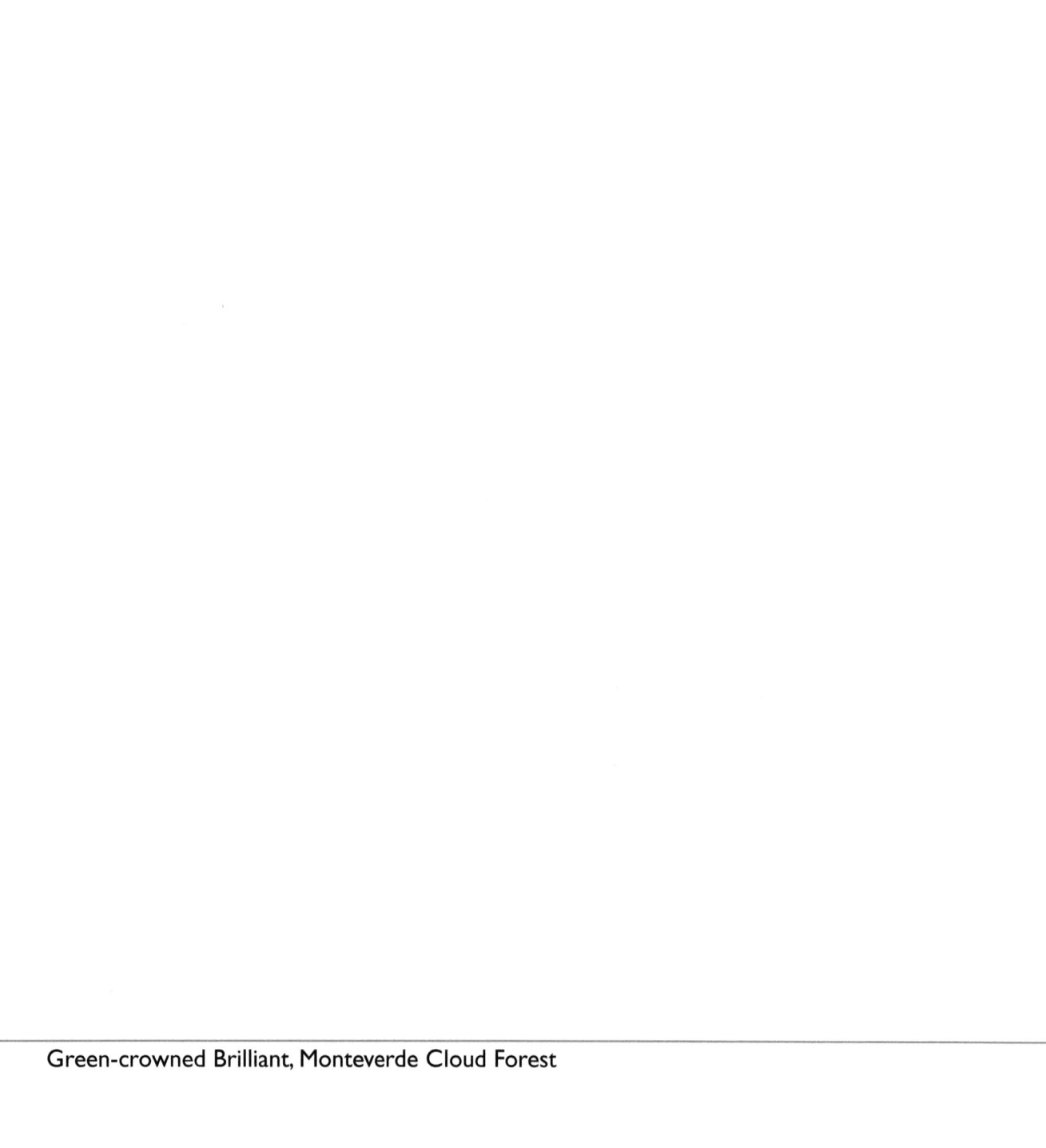

Green-crowned Brilliant, Monteverde Cloud Forest

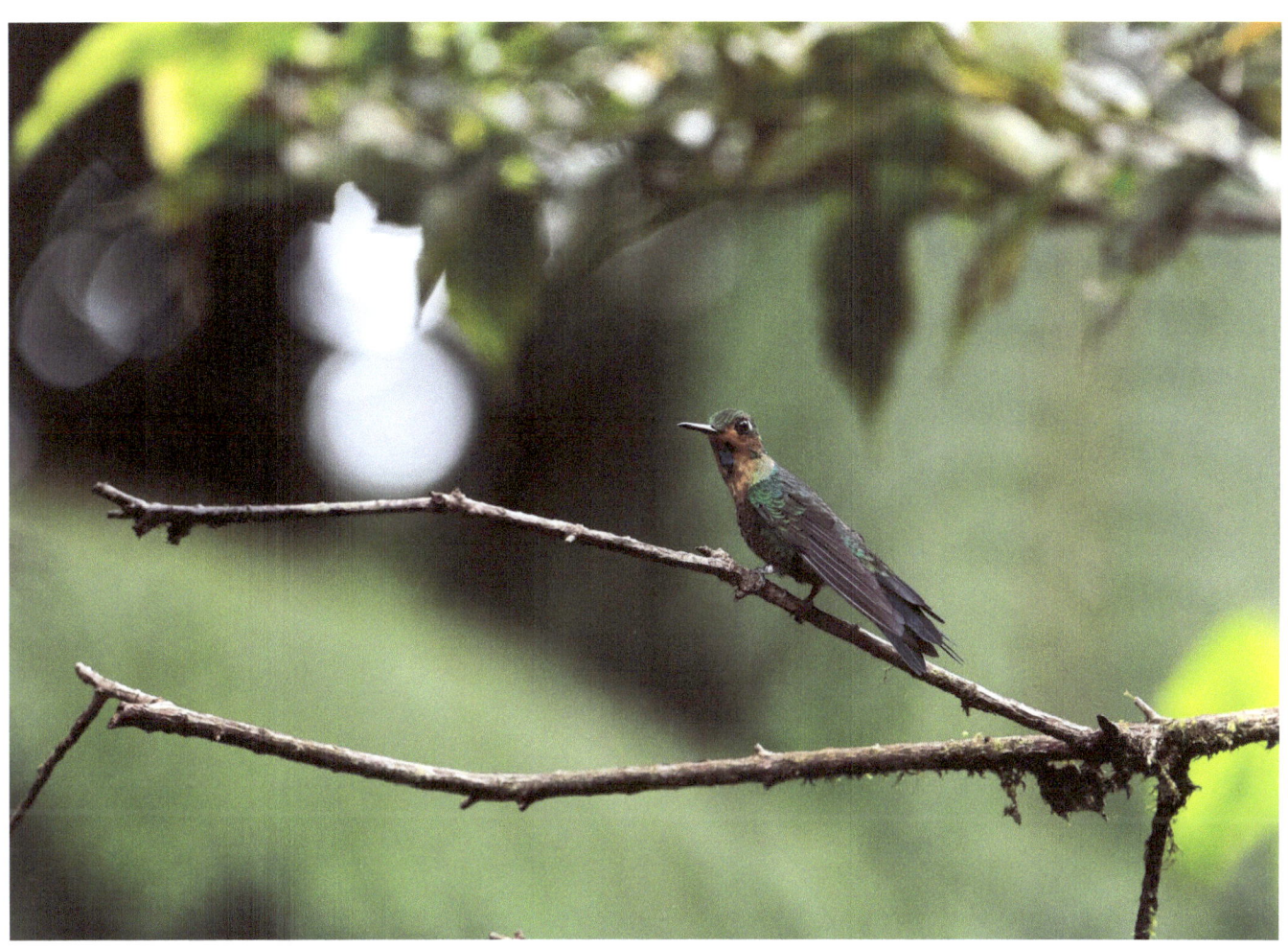

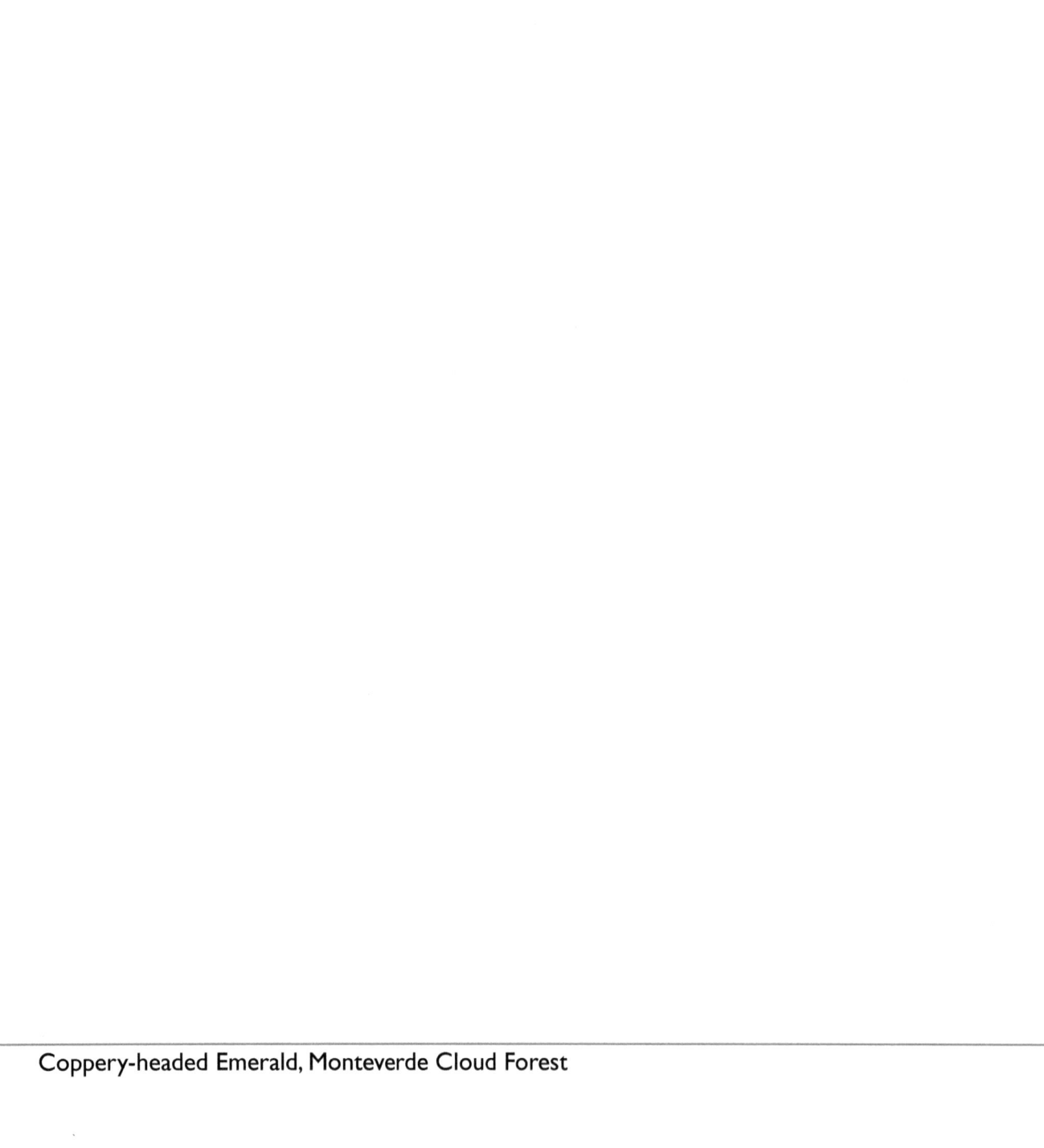

Coppery-headed Emerald, Monteverde Cloud Forest

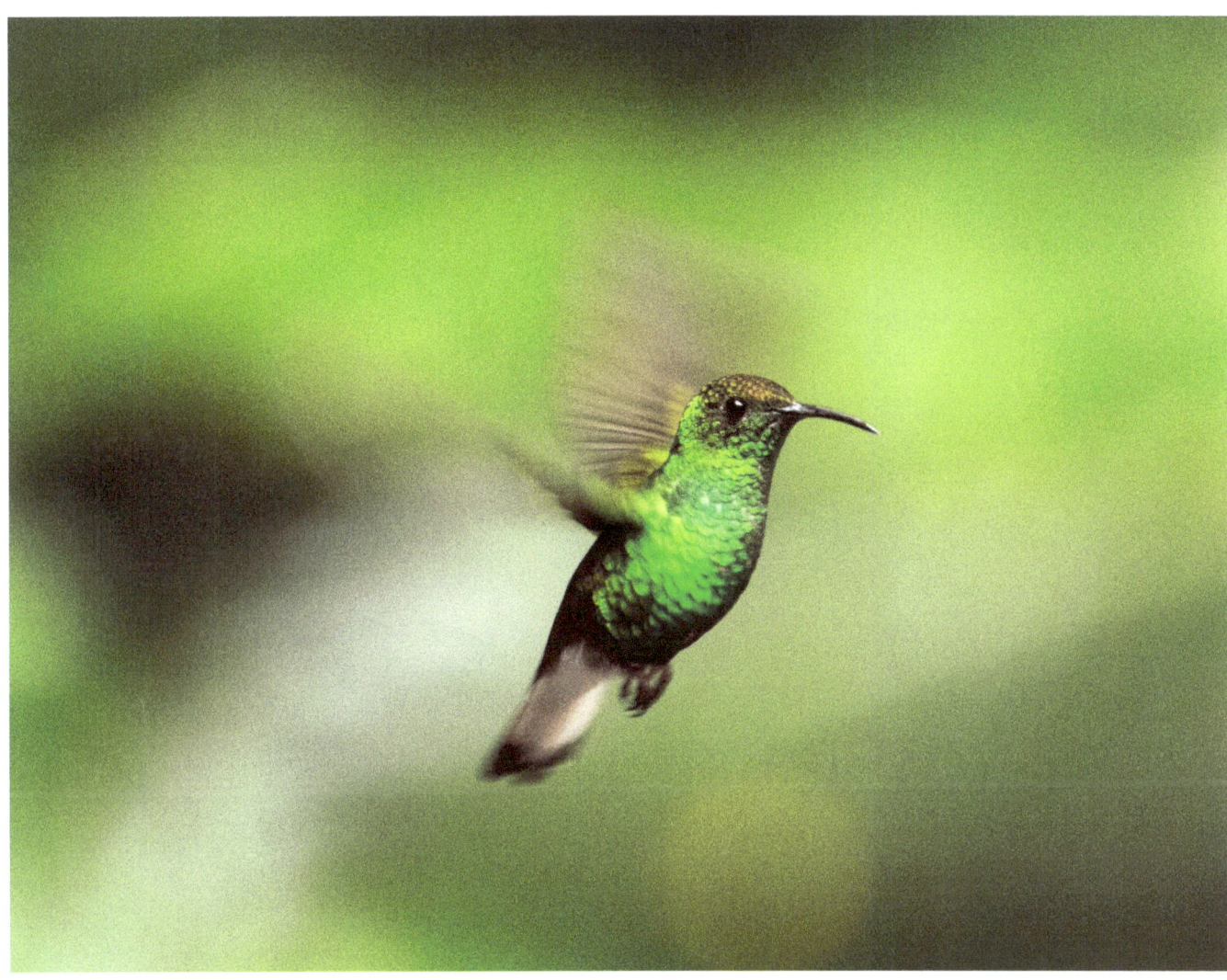

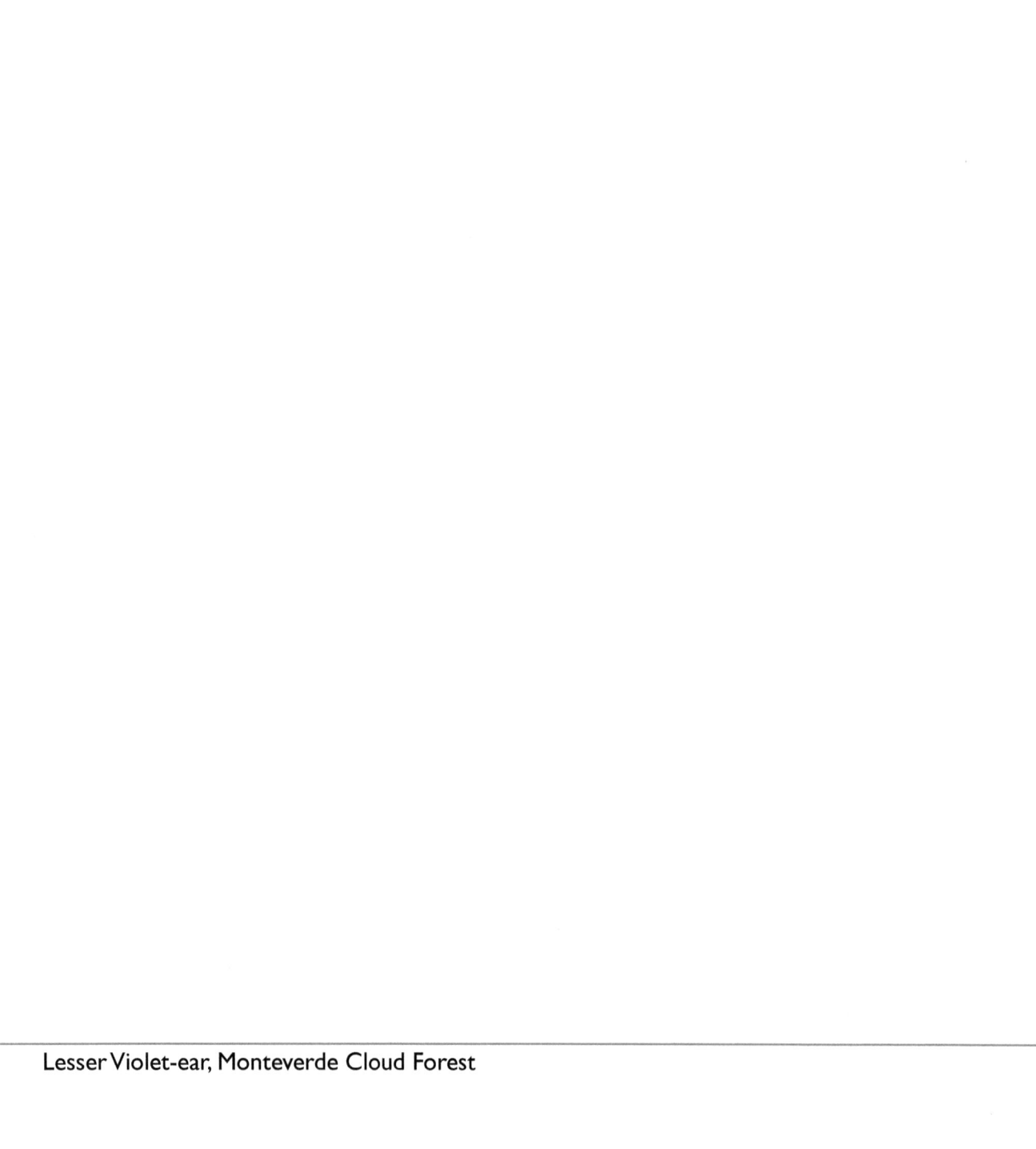

Lesser Violet-ear, Monteverde Cloud Forest

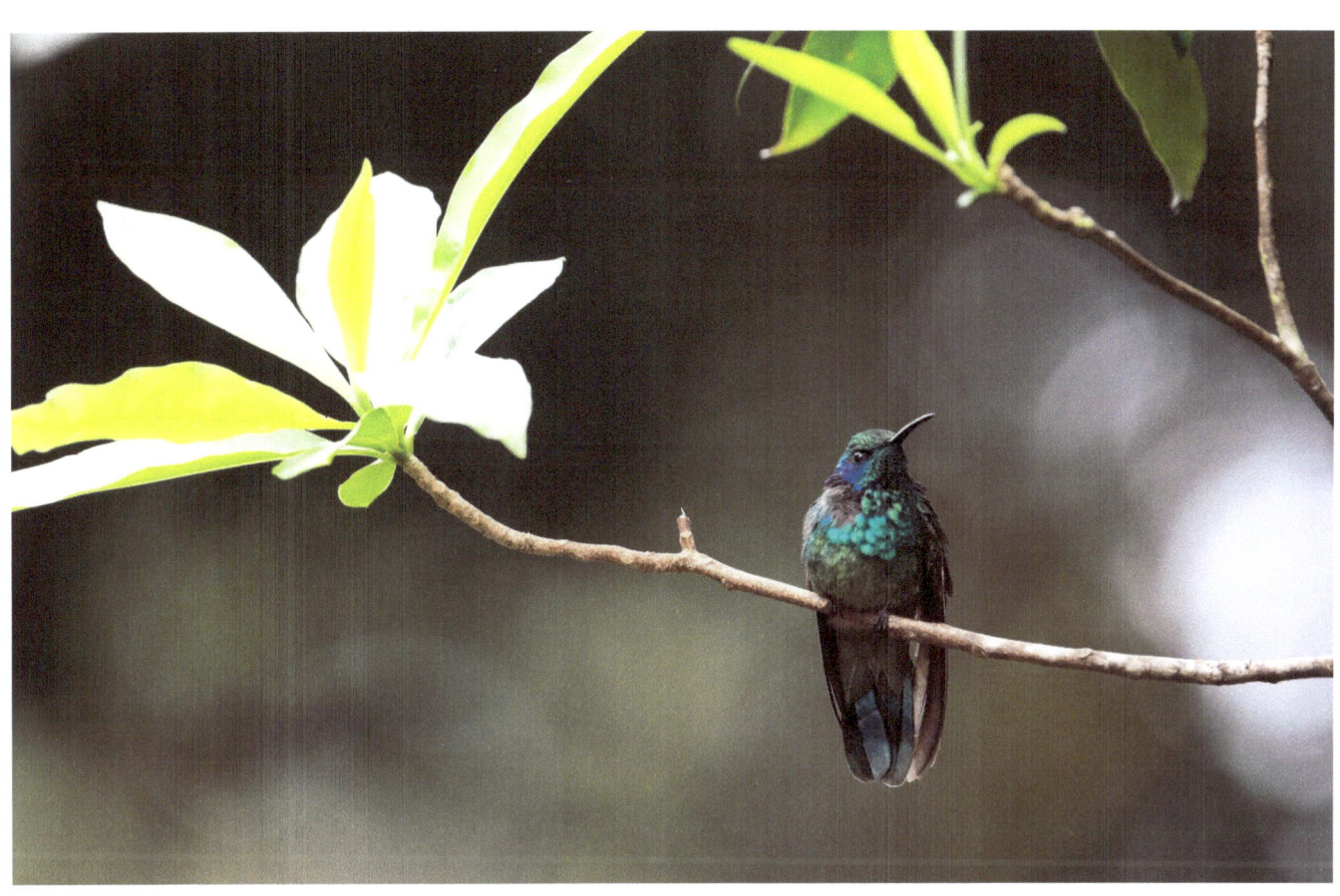

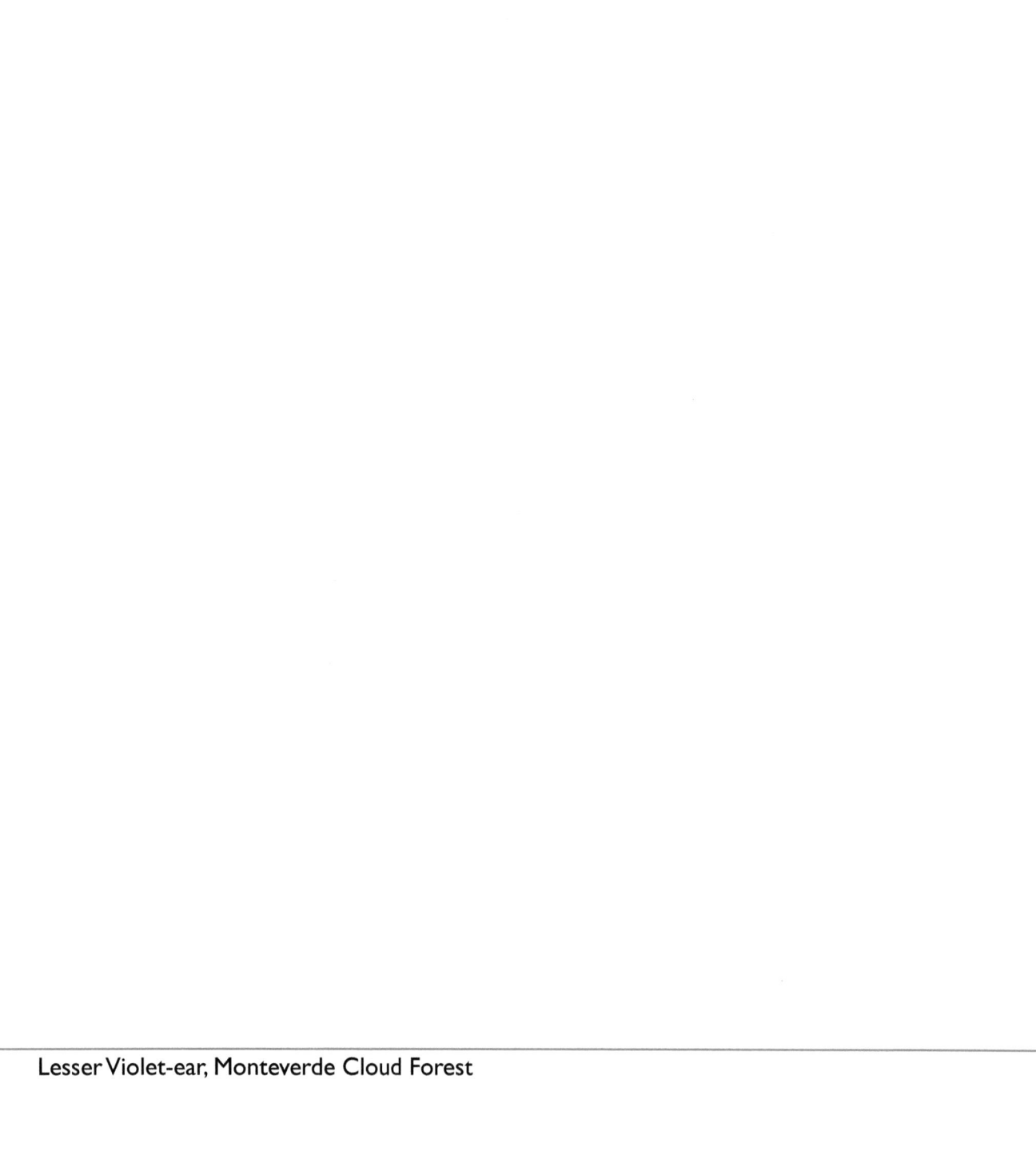

Lesser Violet-ear, Monteverde Cloud Forest

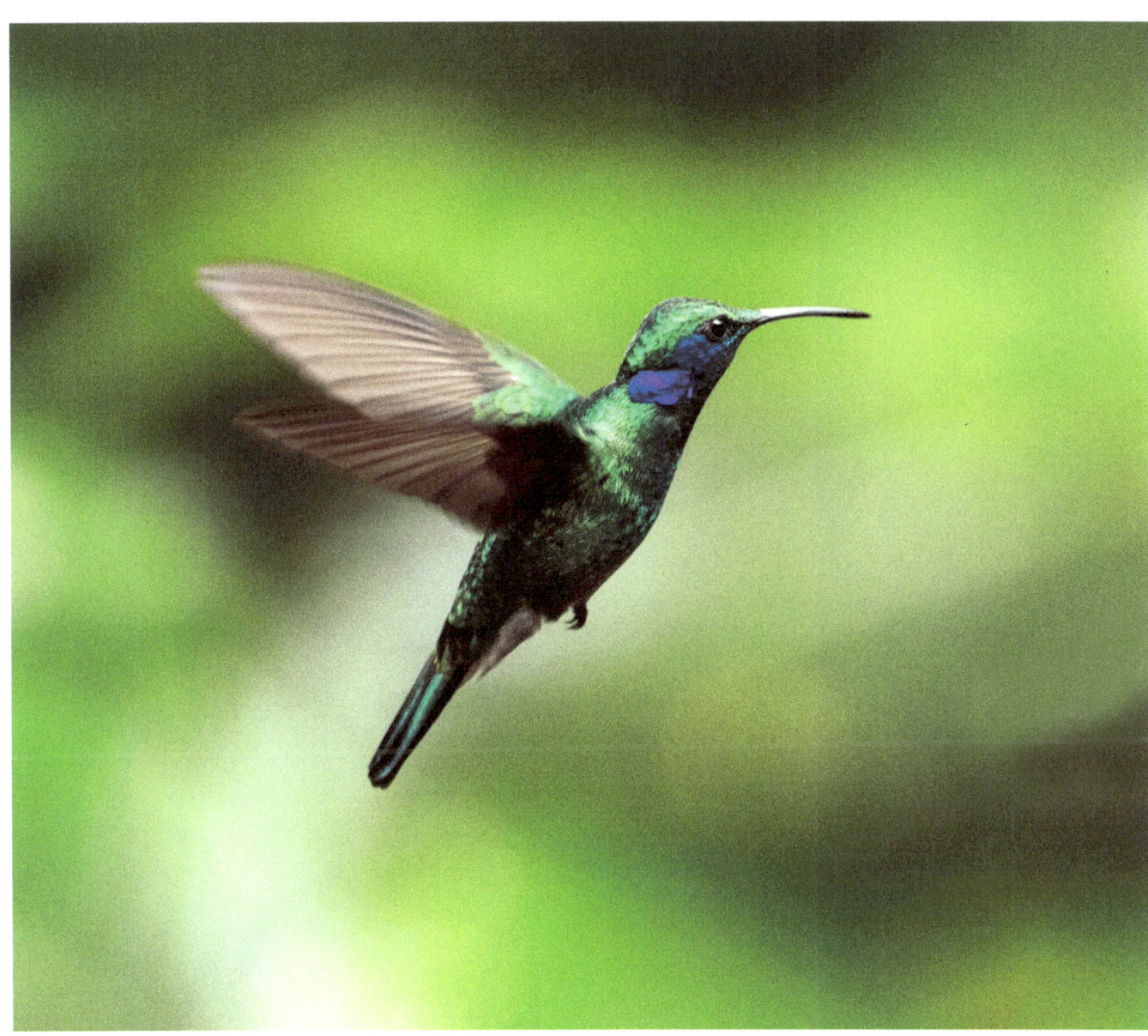

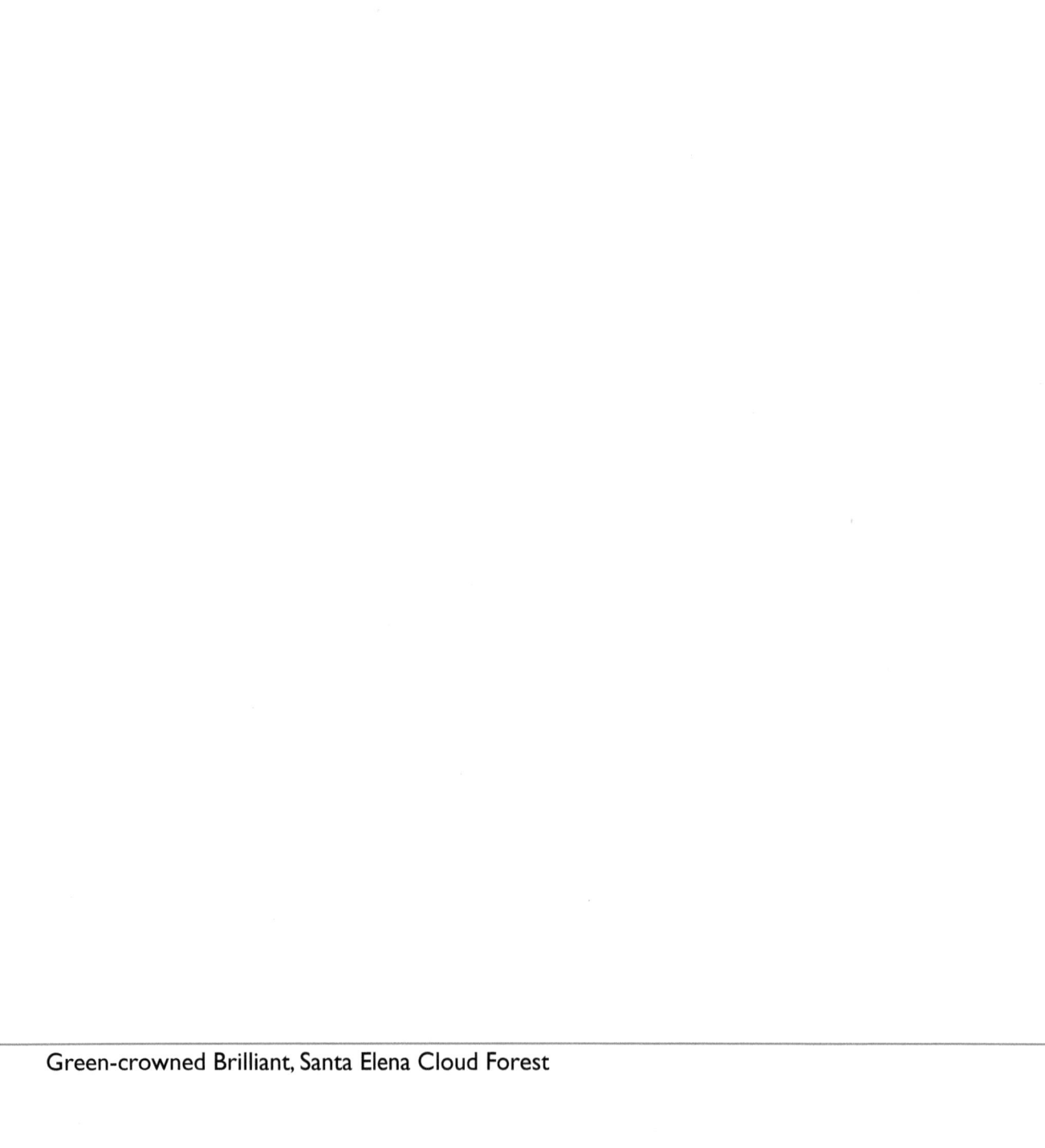

Green-crowned Brilliant, Santa Elena Cloud Forest

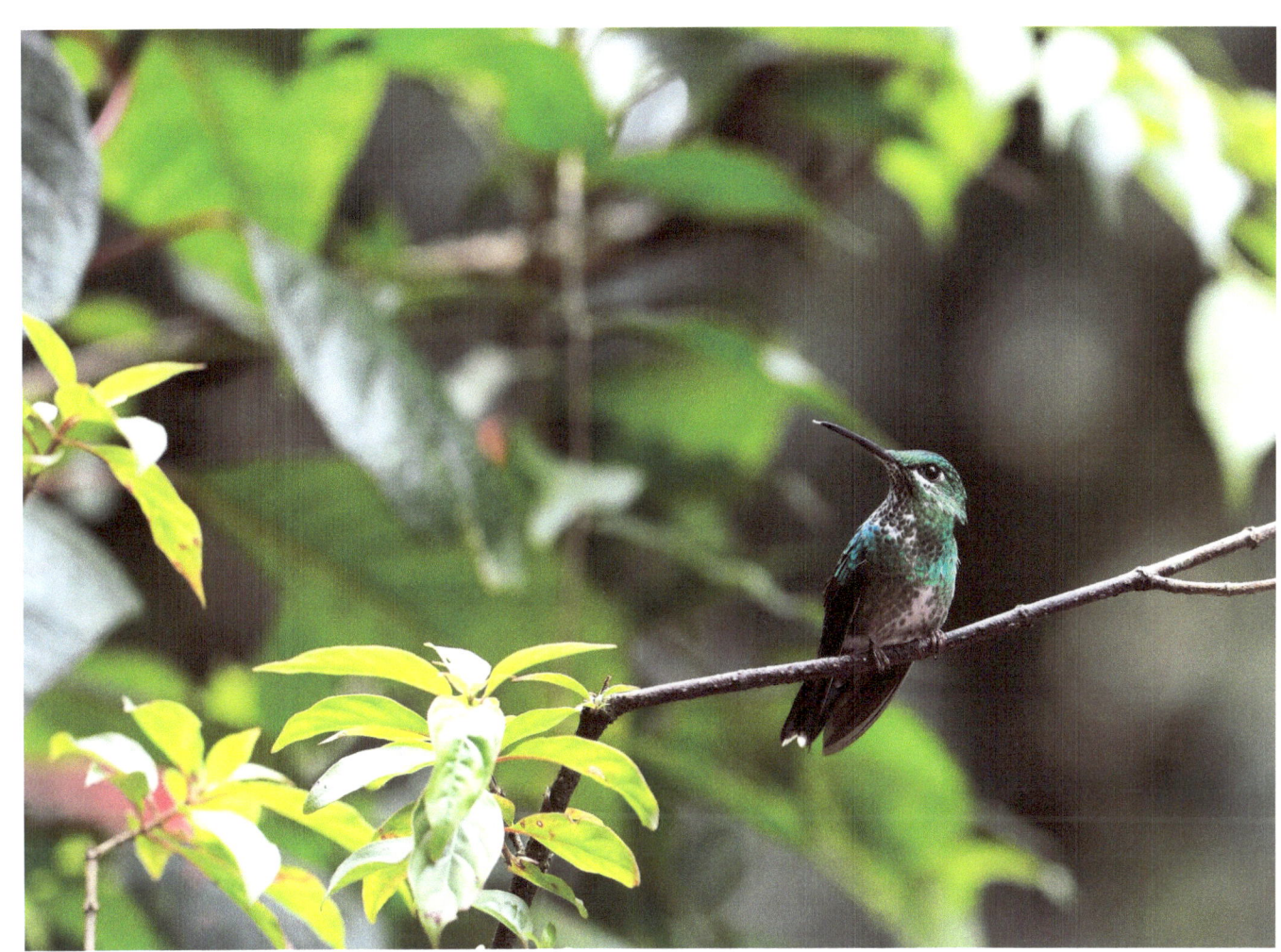

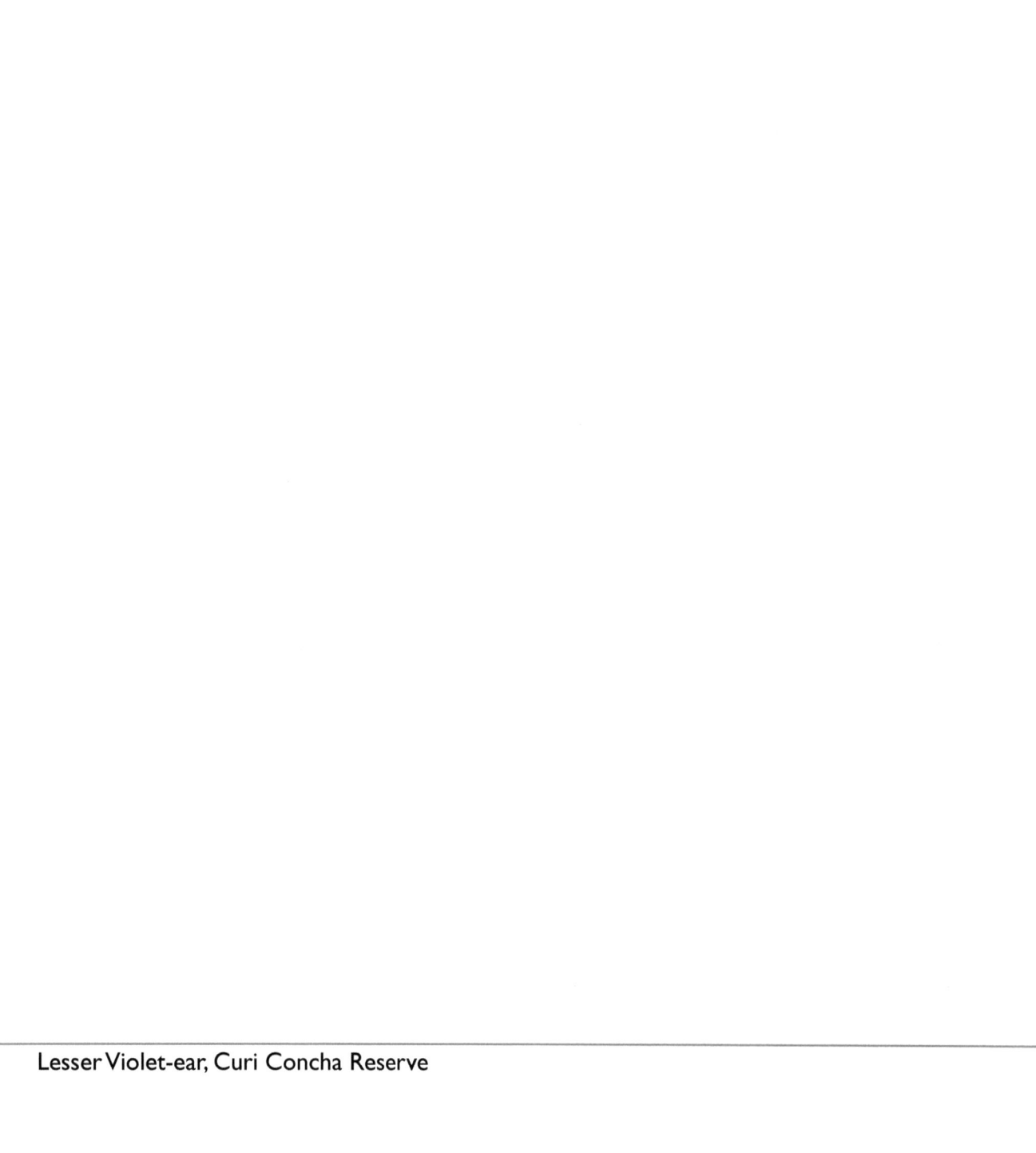

Lesser Violet-ear, Curi Concha Reserve

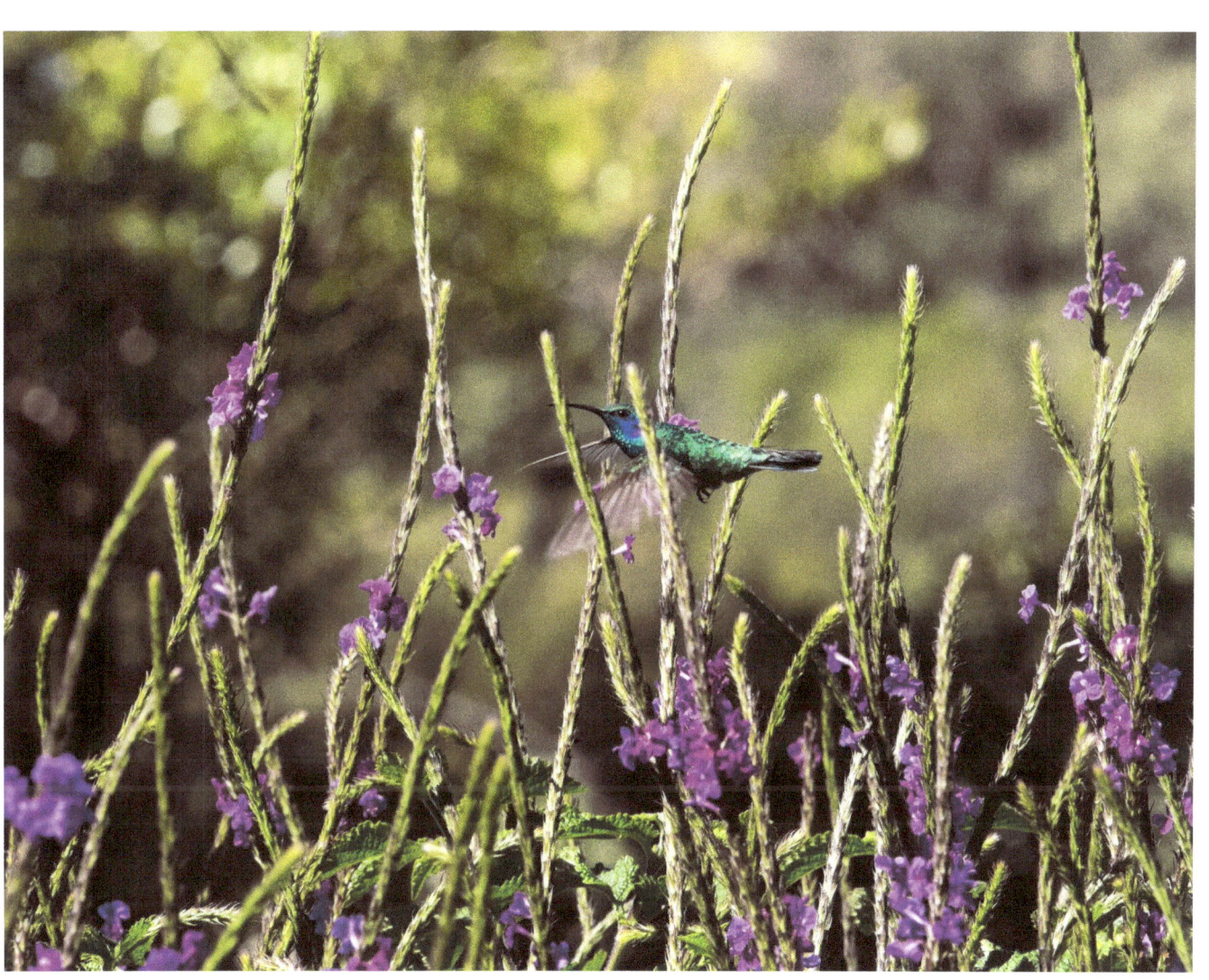

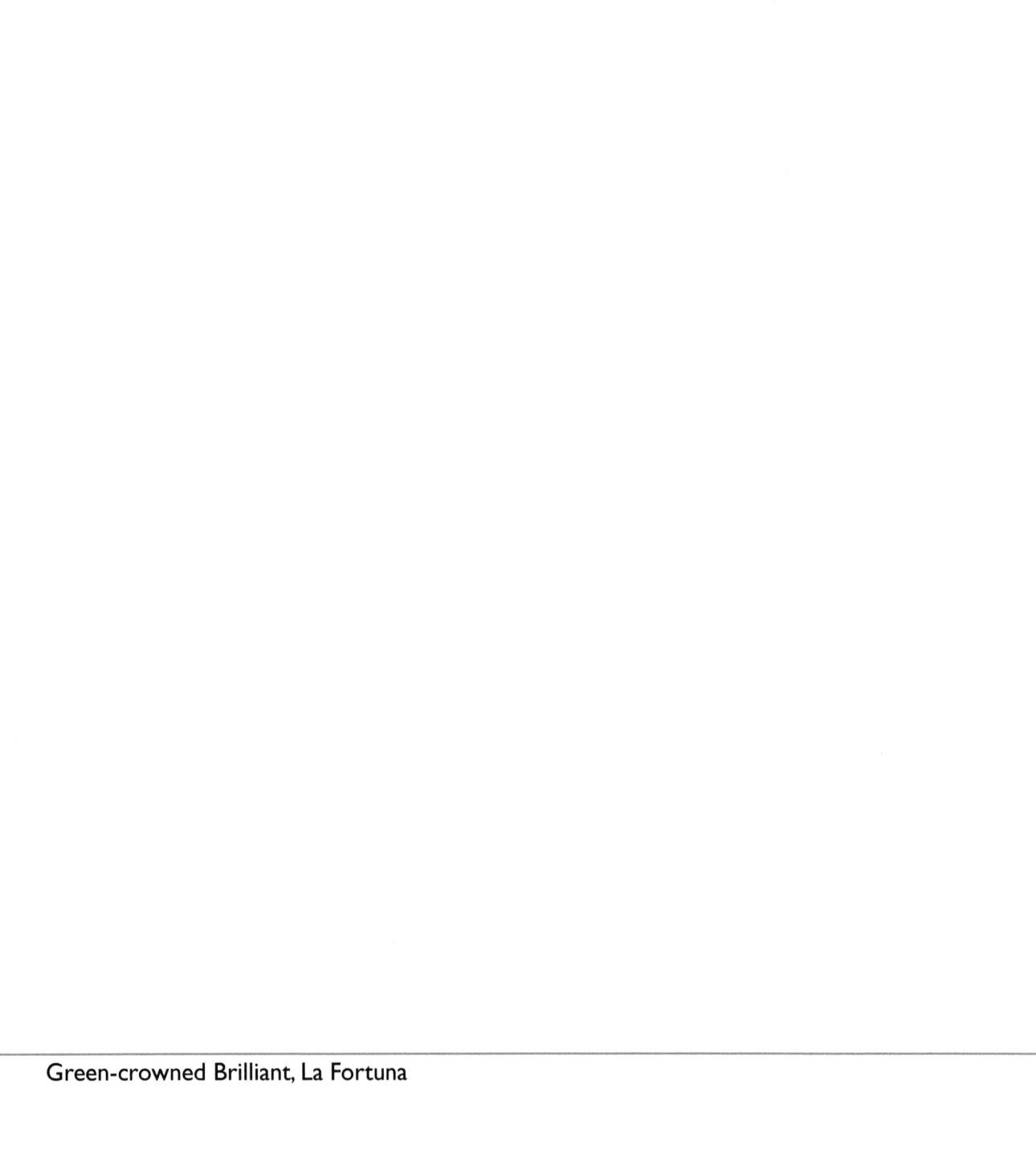

Green-crowned Brilliant, La Fortuna

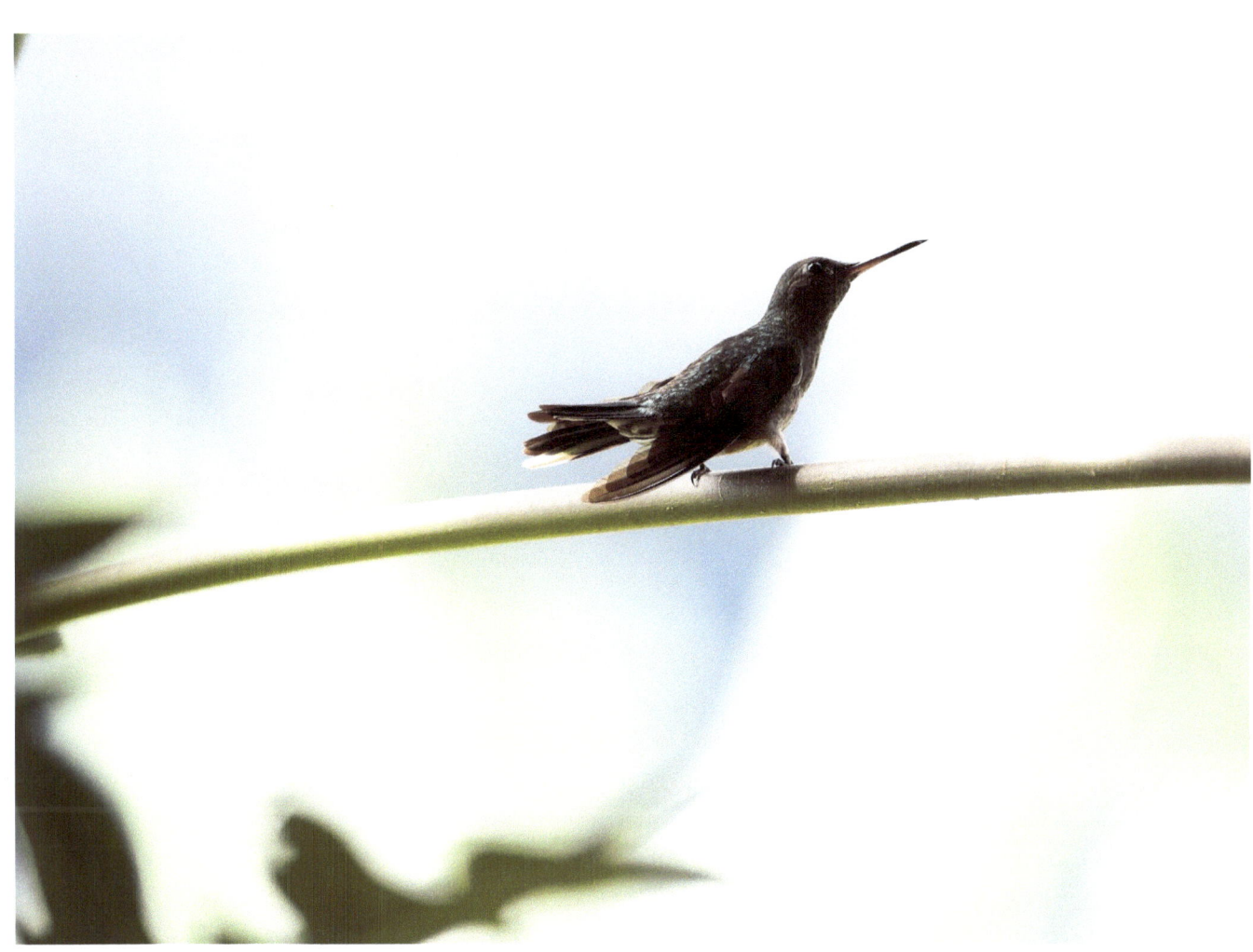

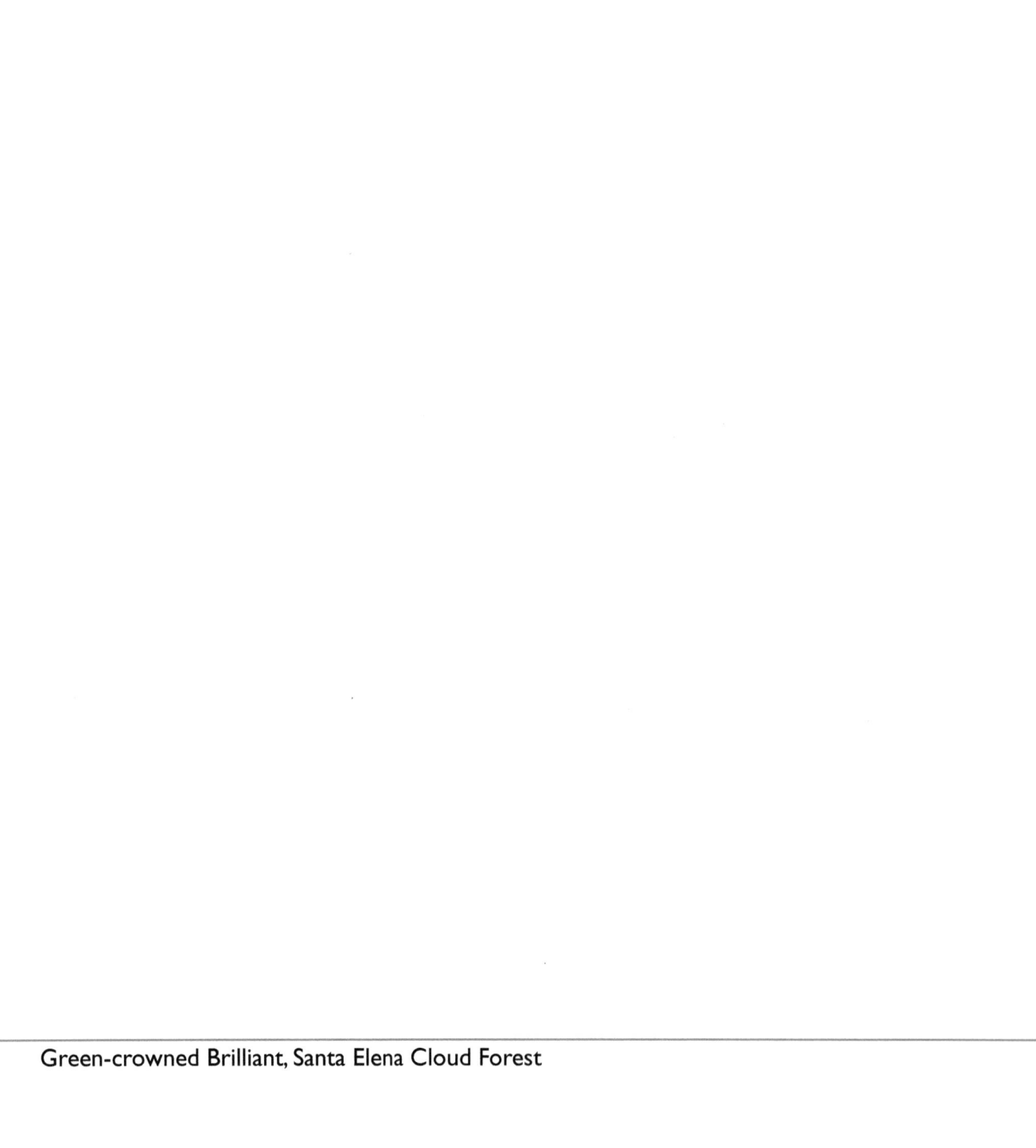

Green-crowned Brilliant, Santa Elena Cloud Forest

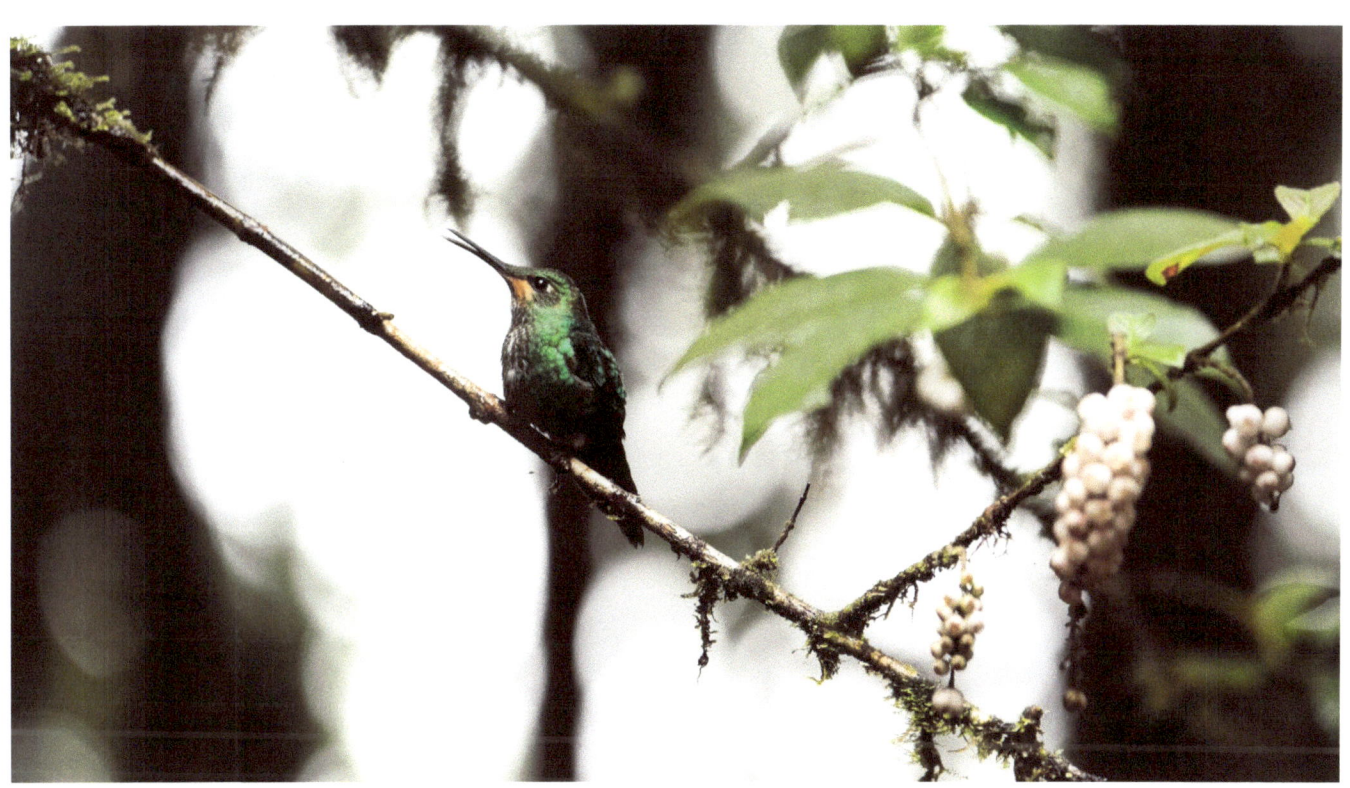

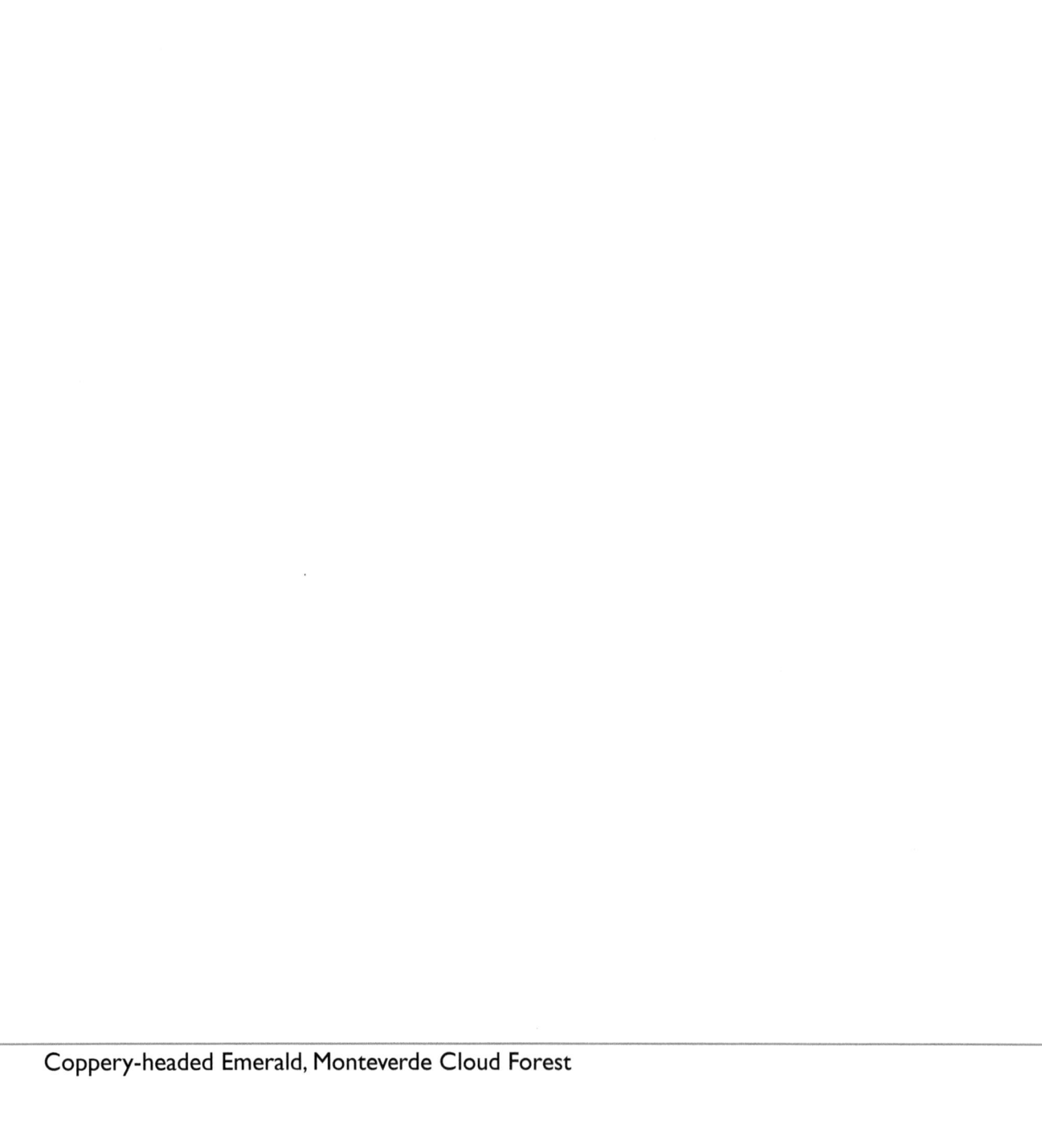

Coppery-headed Emerald, Monteverde Cloud Forest

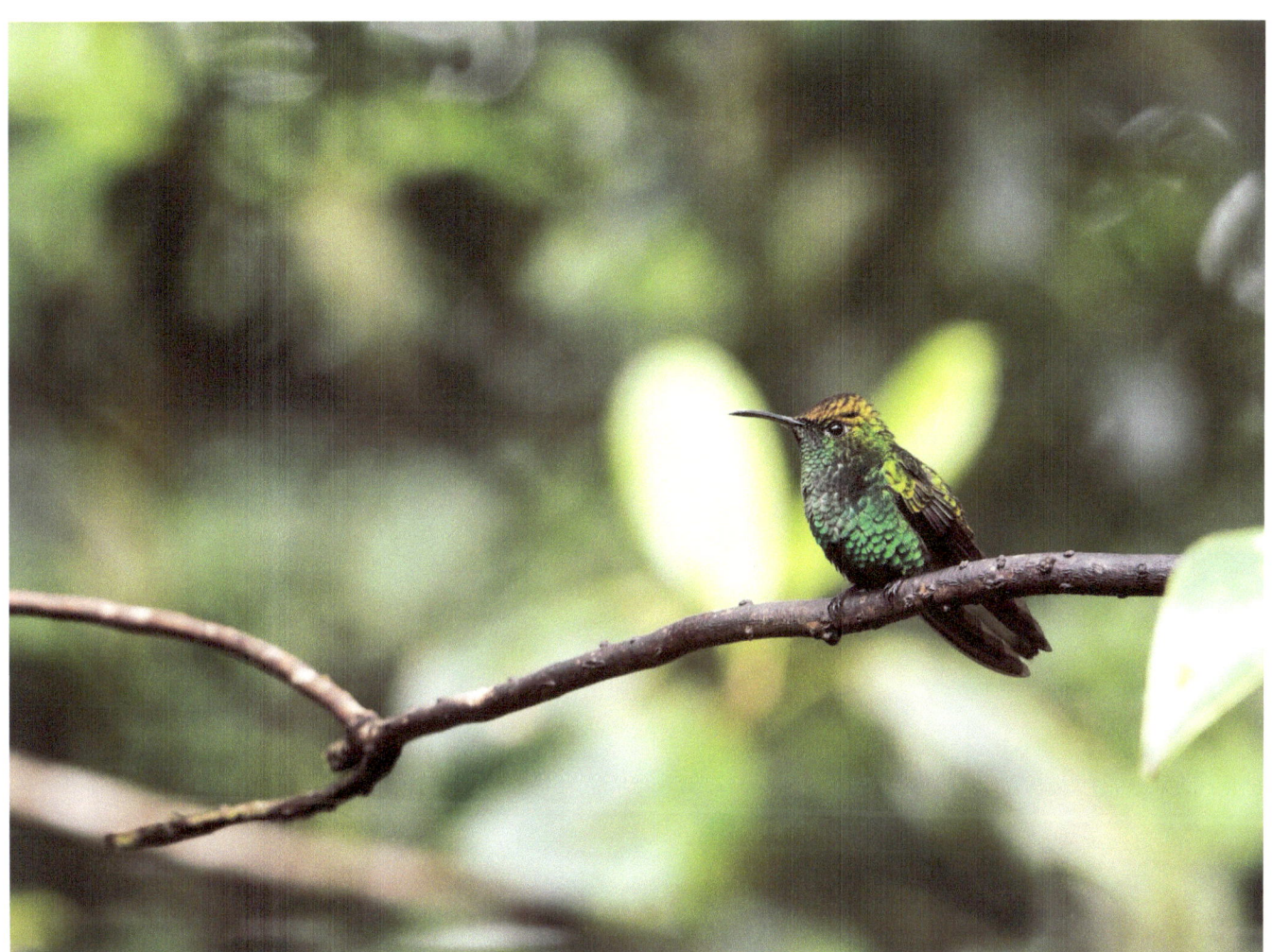

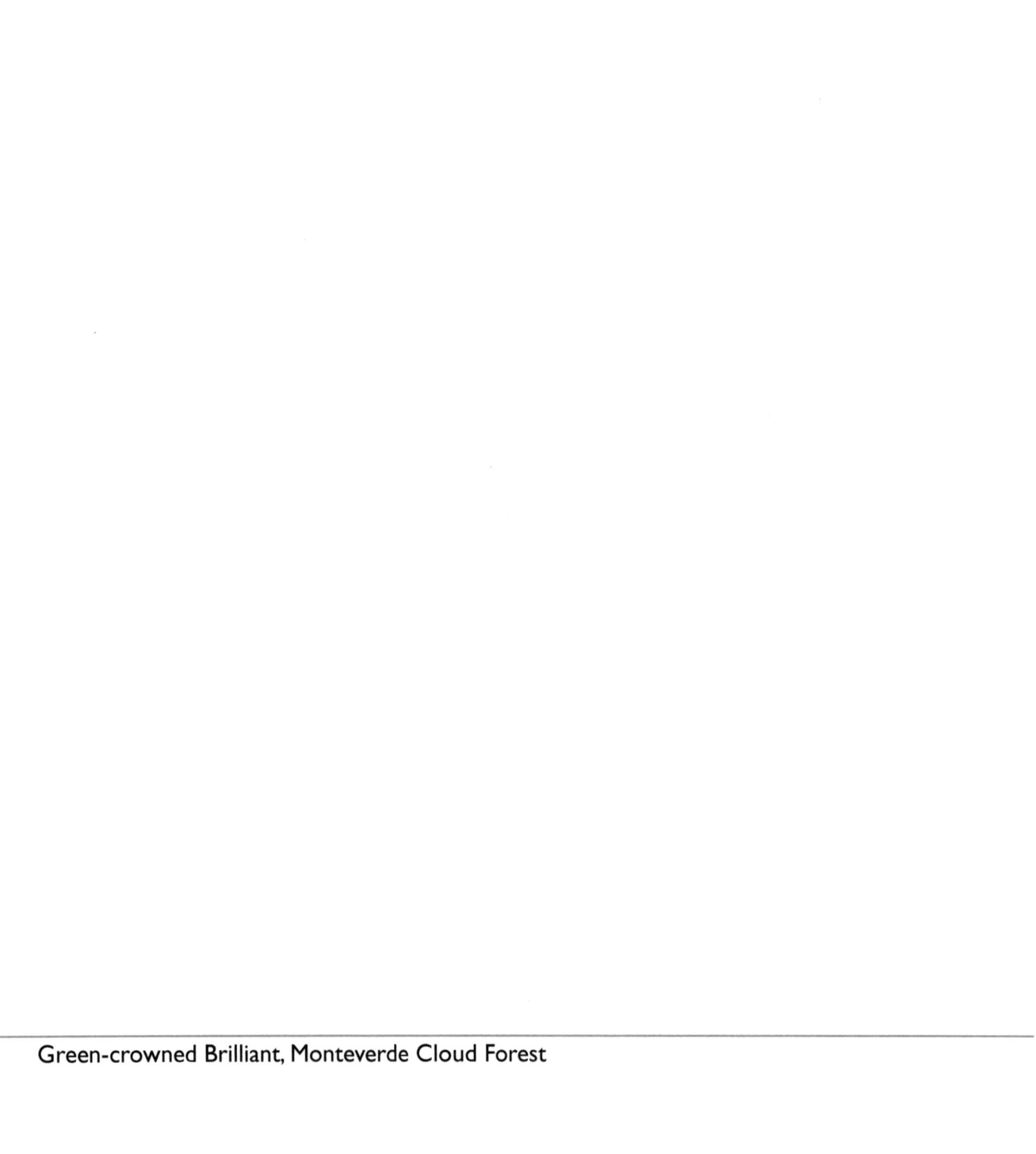

Green-crowned Brilliant, Monteverde Cloud Forest

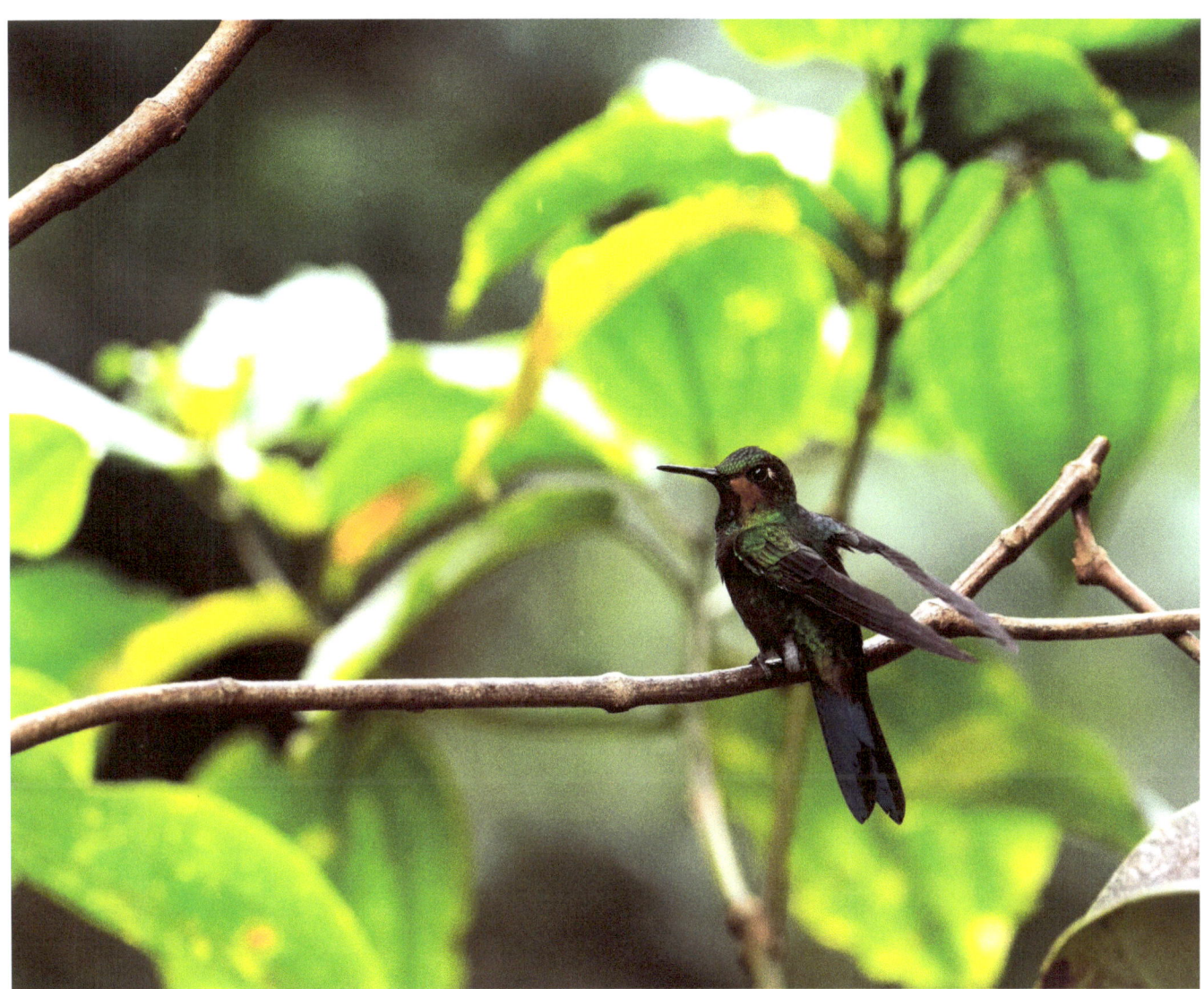

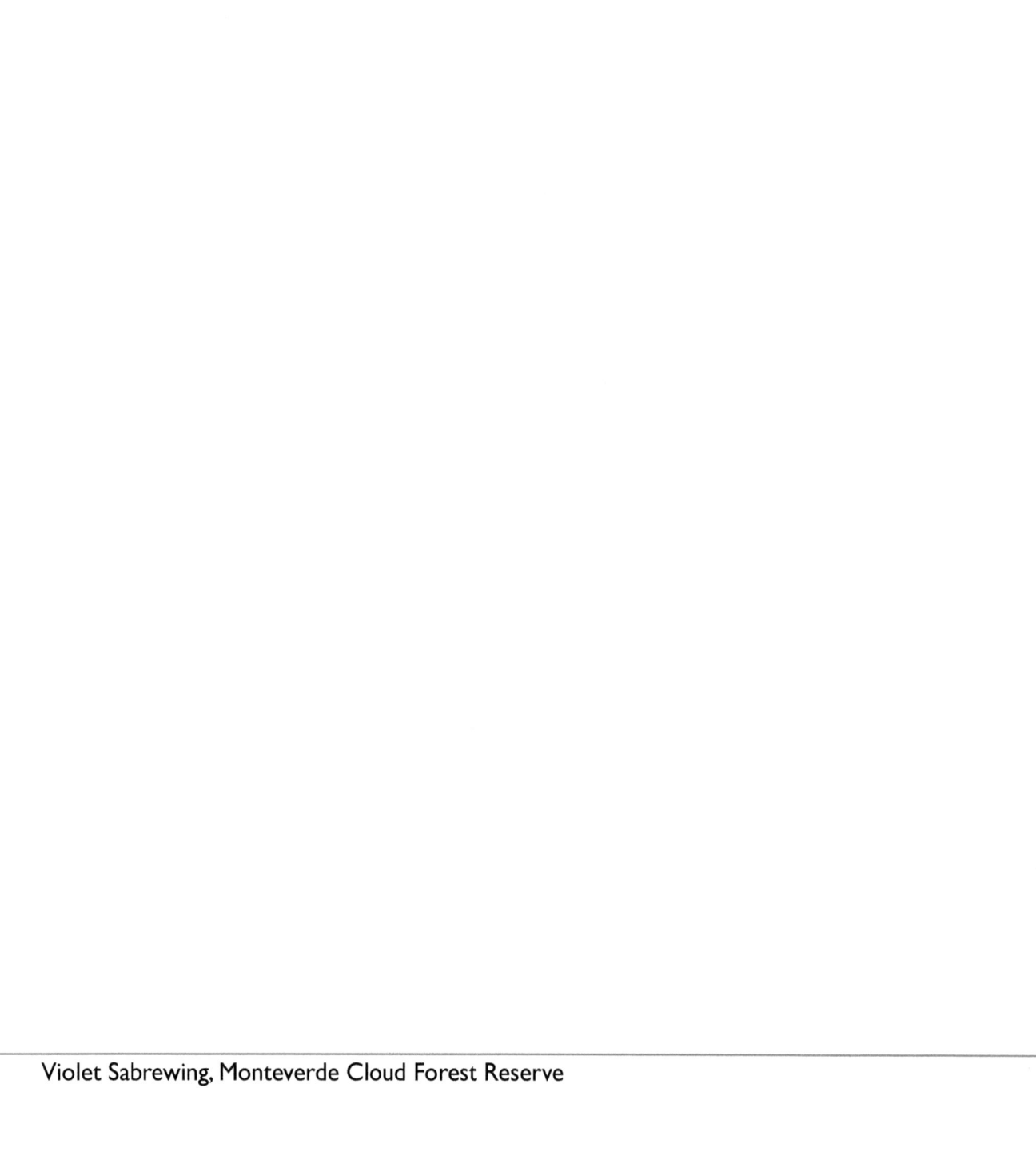

Violet Sabrewing, Monteverde Cloud Forest Reserve

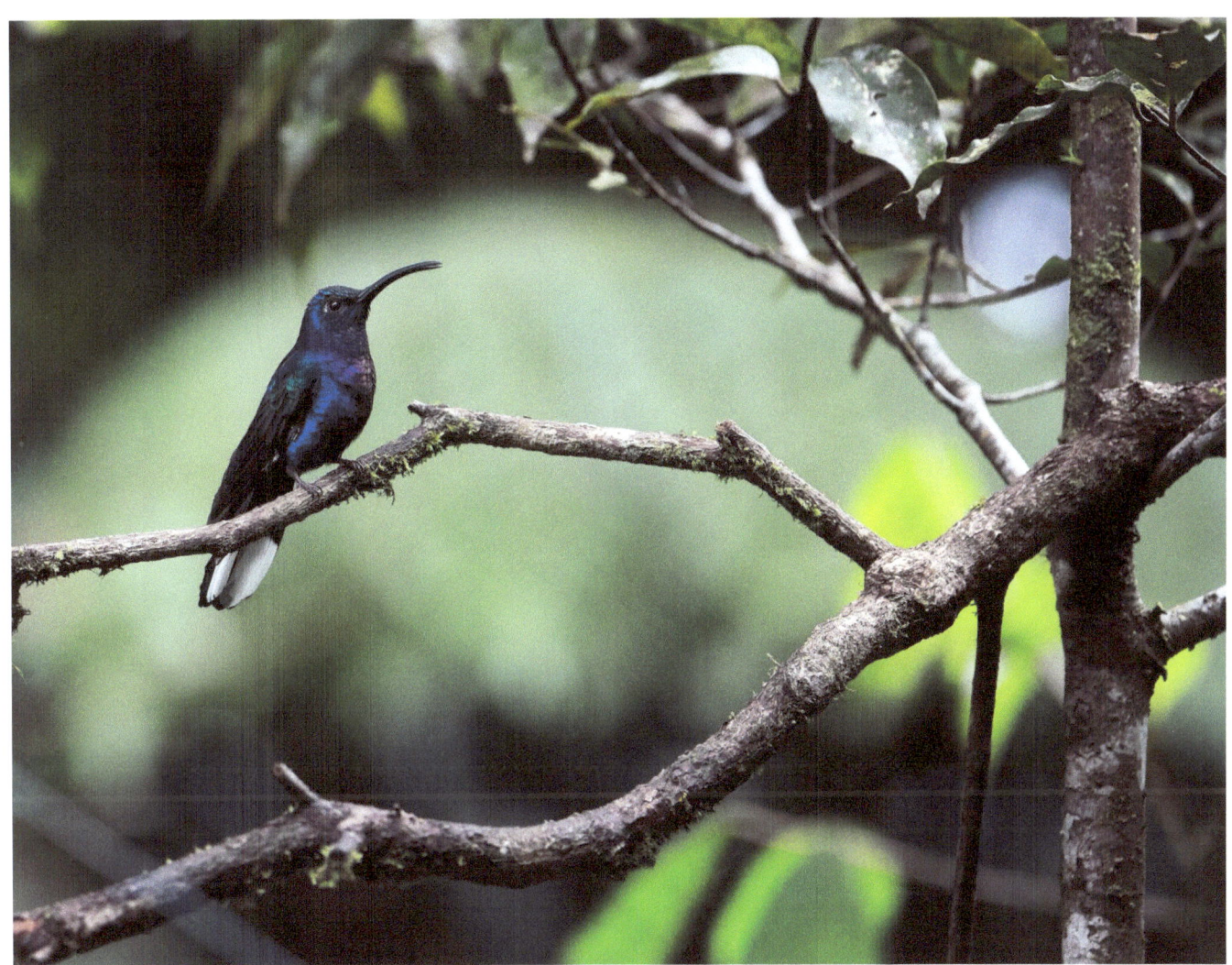

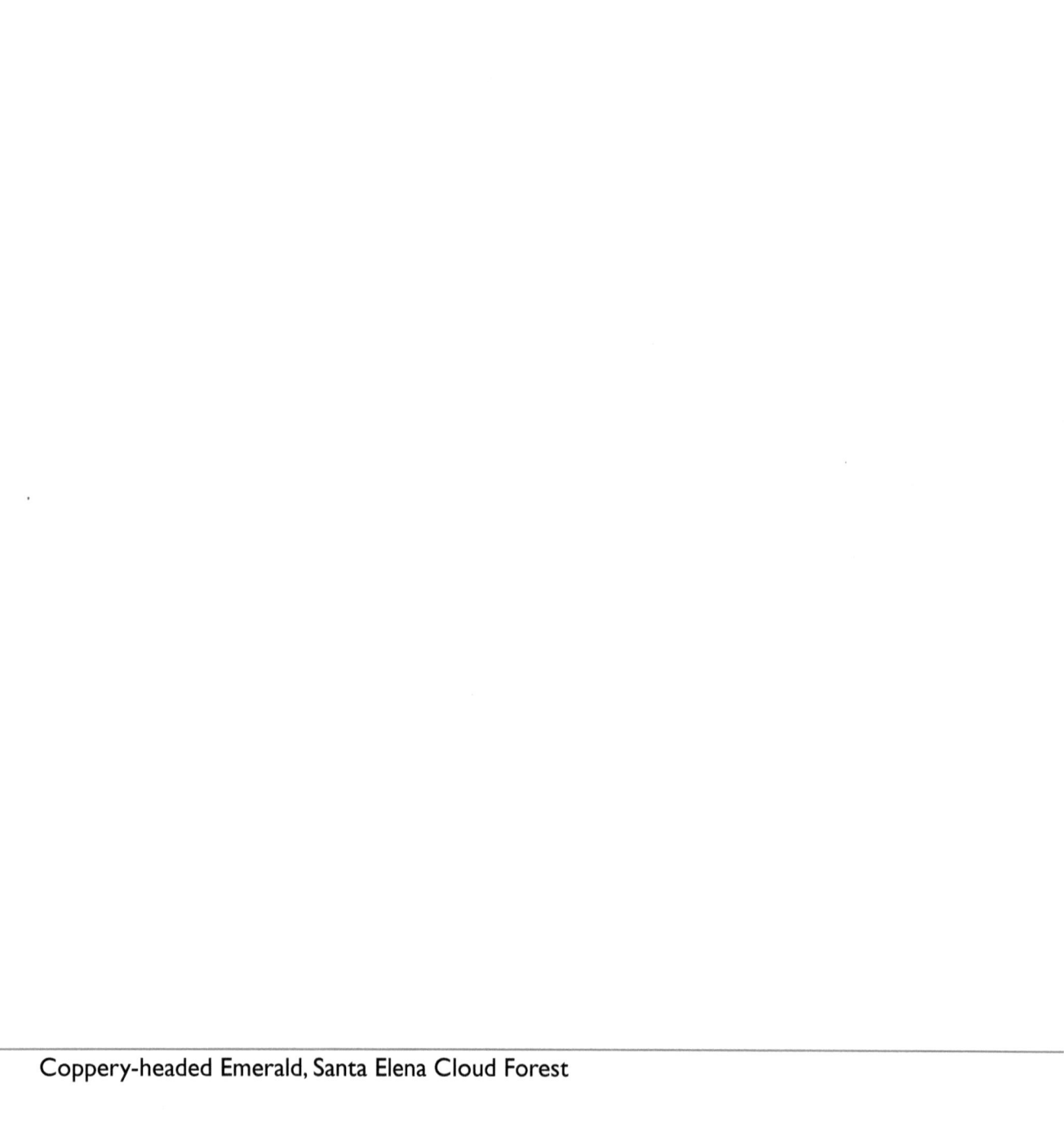

Coppery-headed Emerald, Santa Elena Cloud Forest

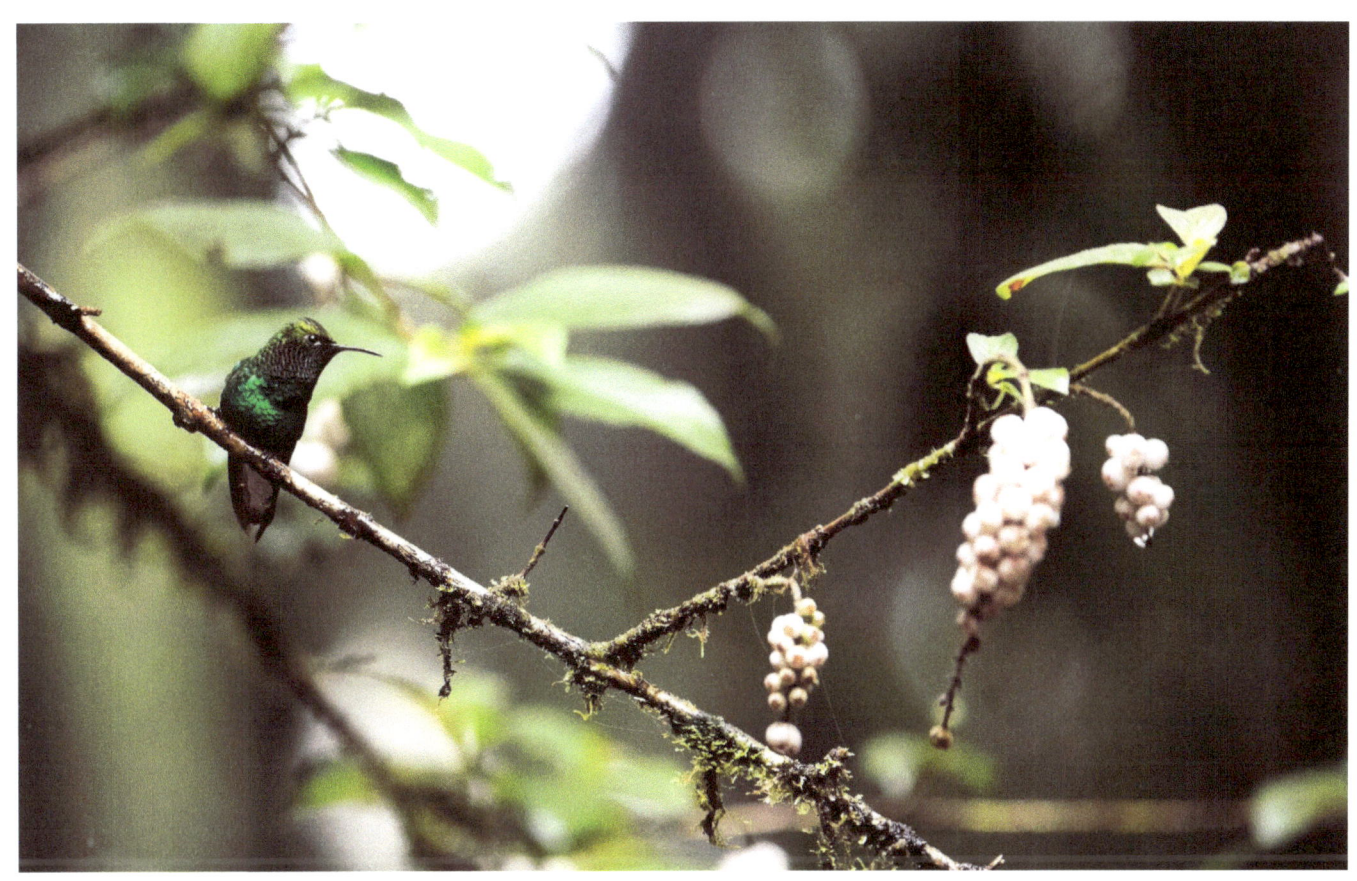

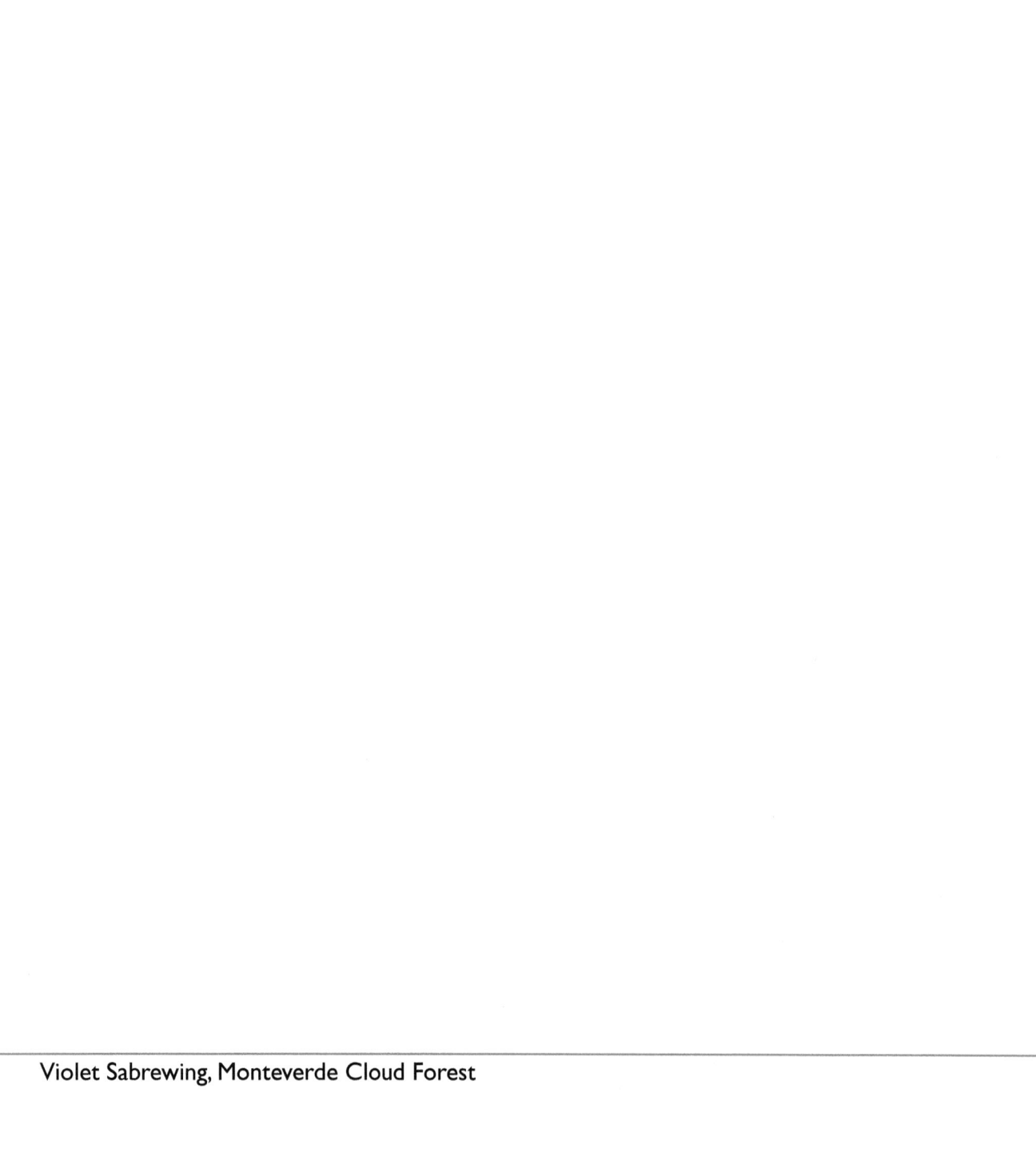

Violet Sabrewing, Monteverde Cloud Forest

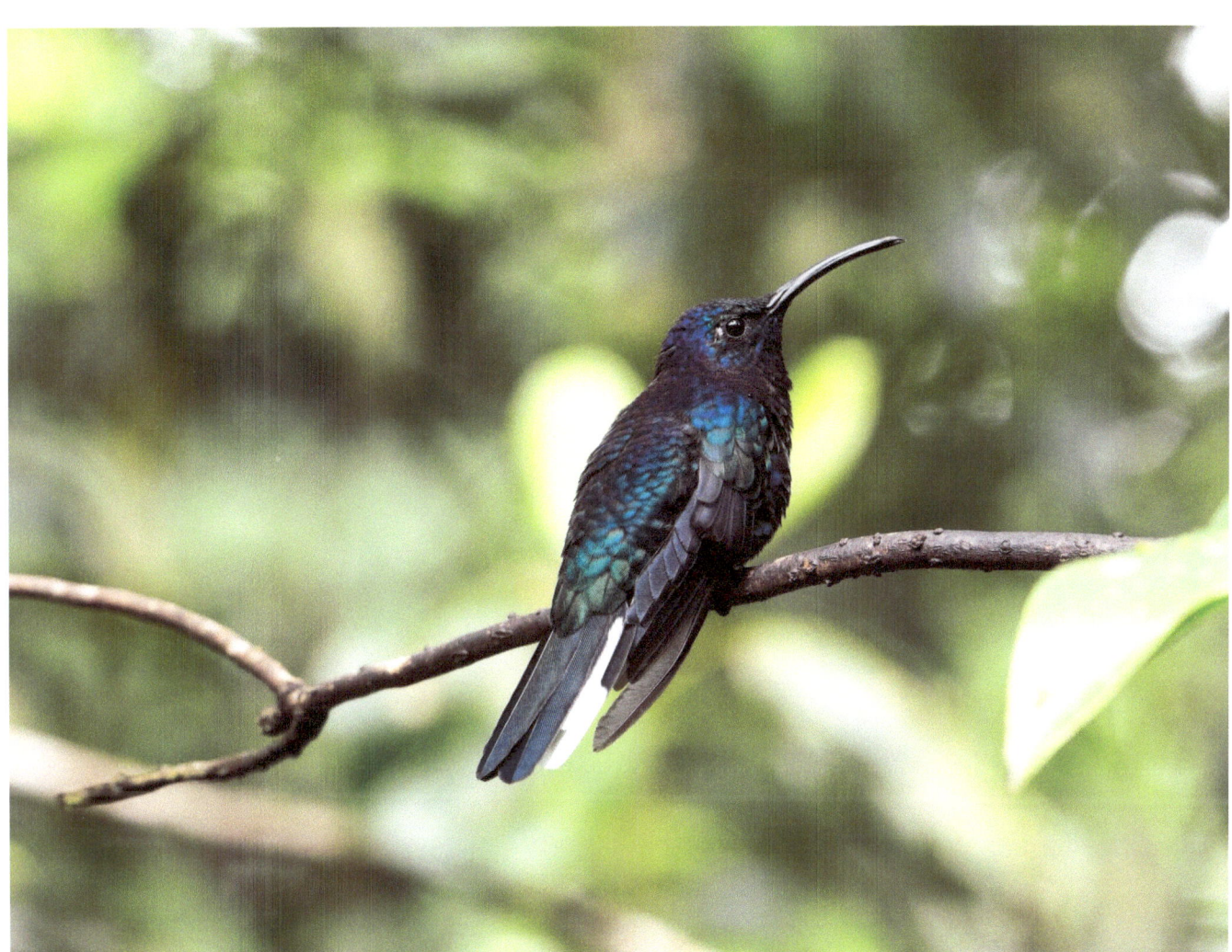

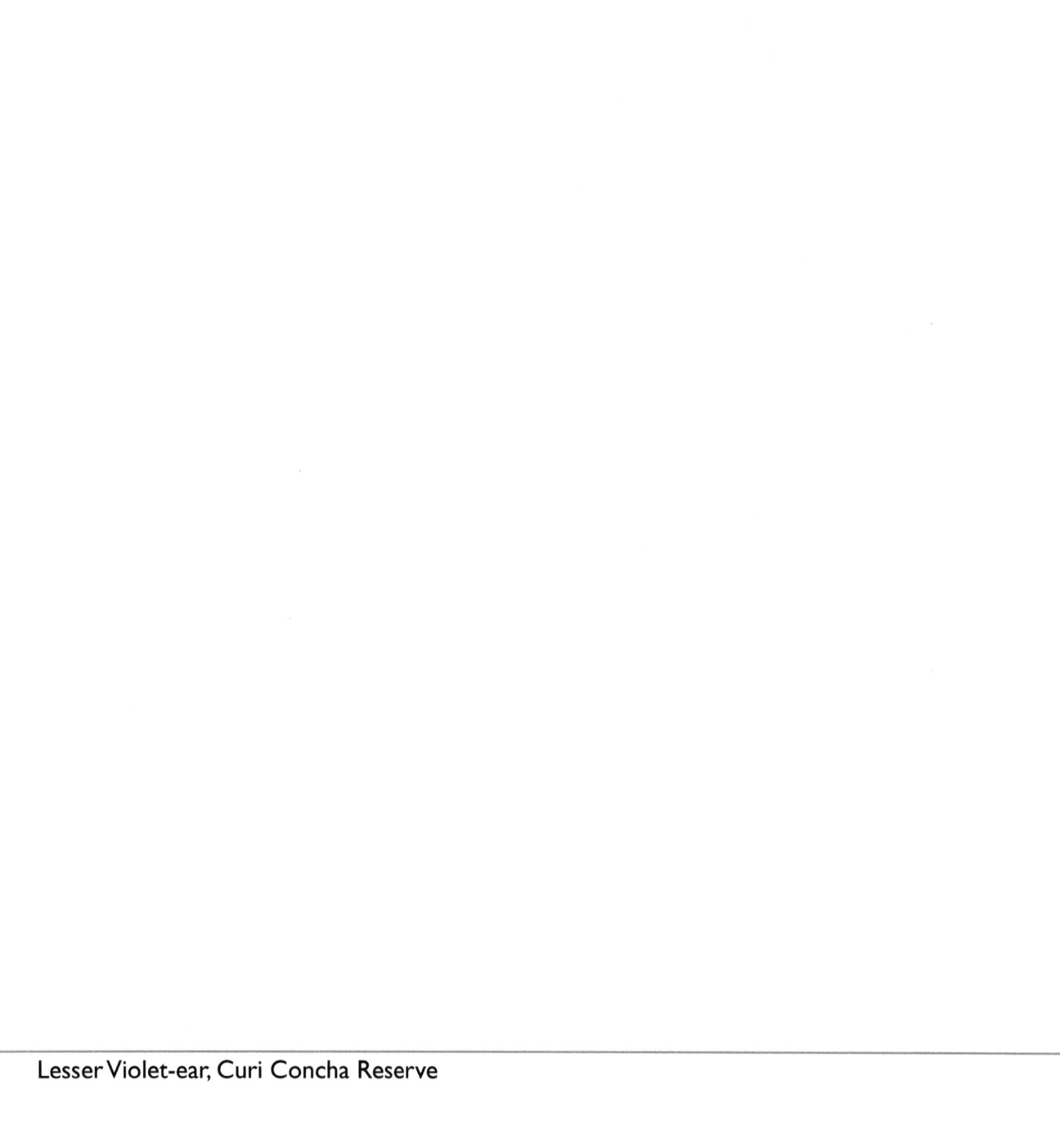

Lesser Violet-ear, Curi Concha Reserve

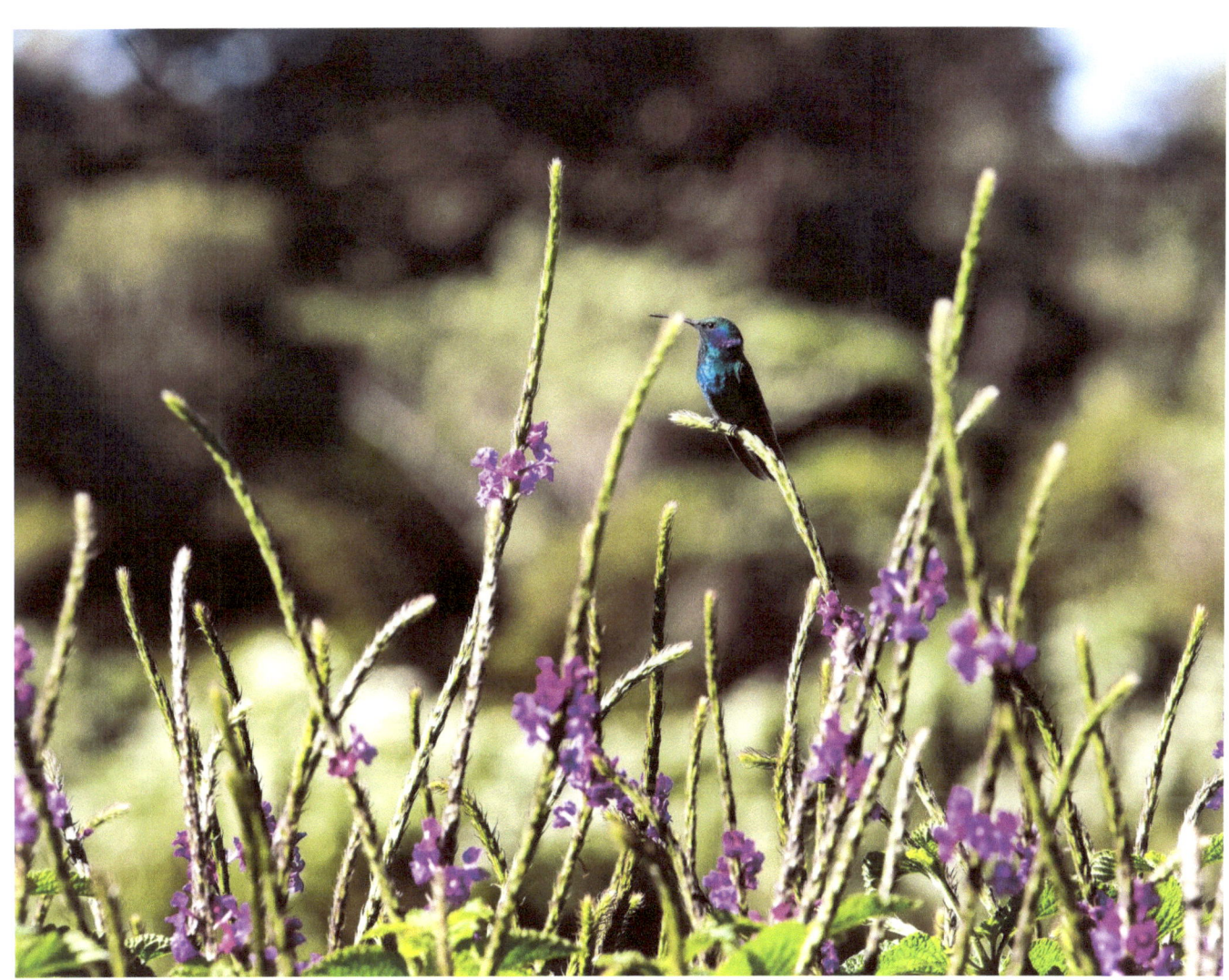

White-necked Jacobin, La Fortuna

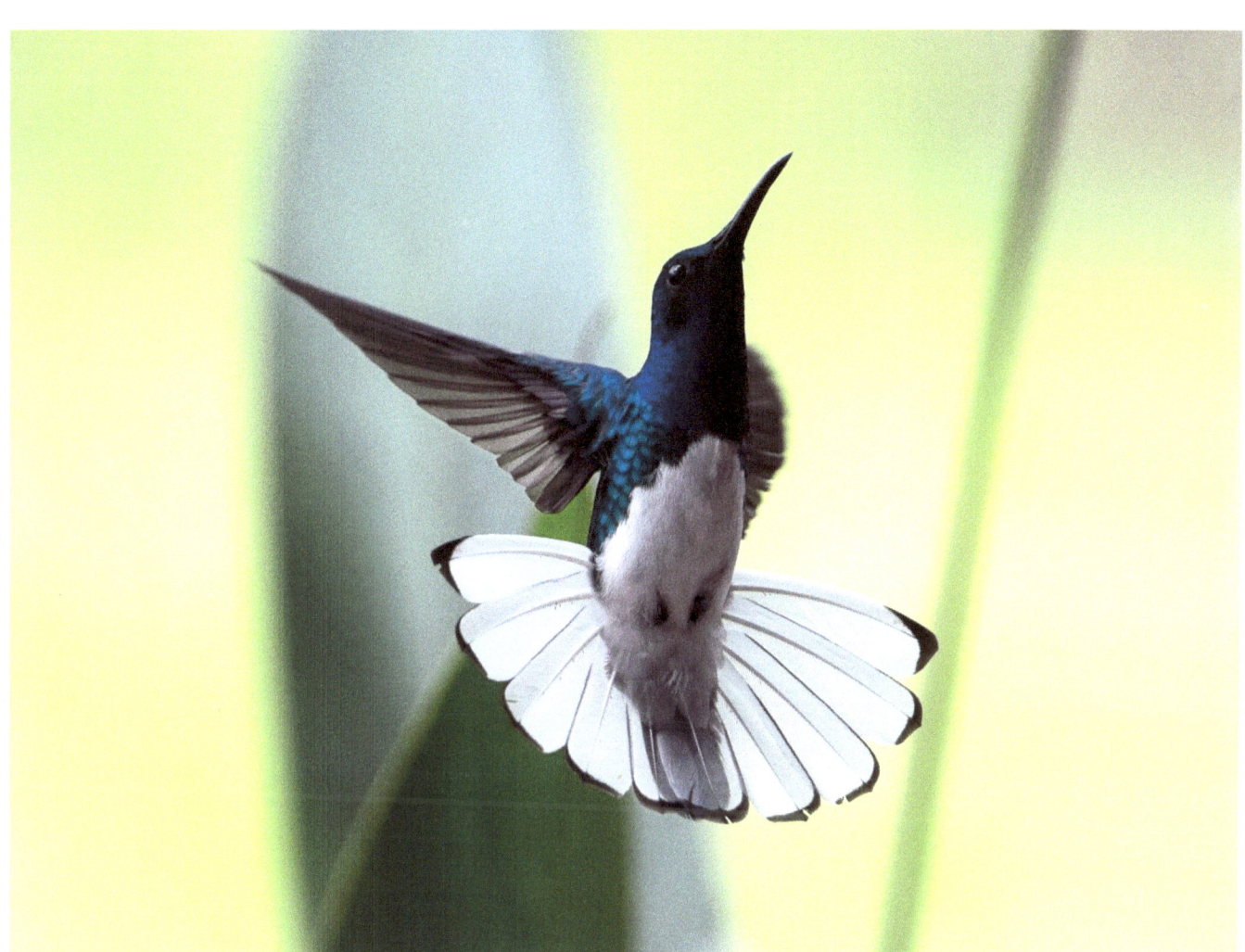

Rufus-tailed Hummingbird, La Fortuna

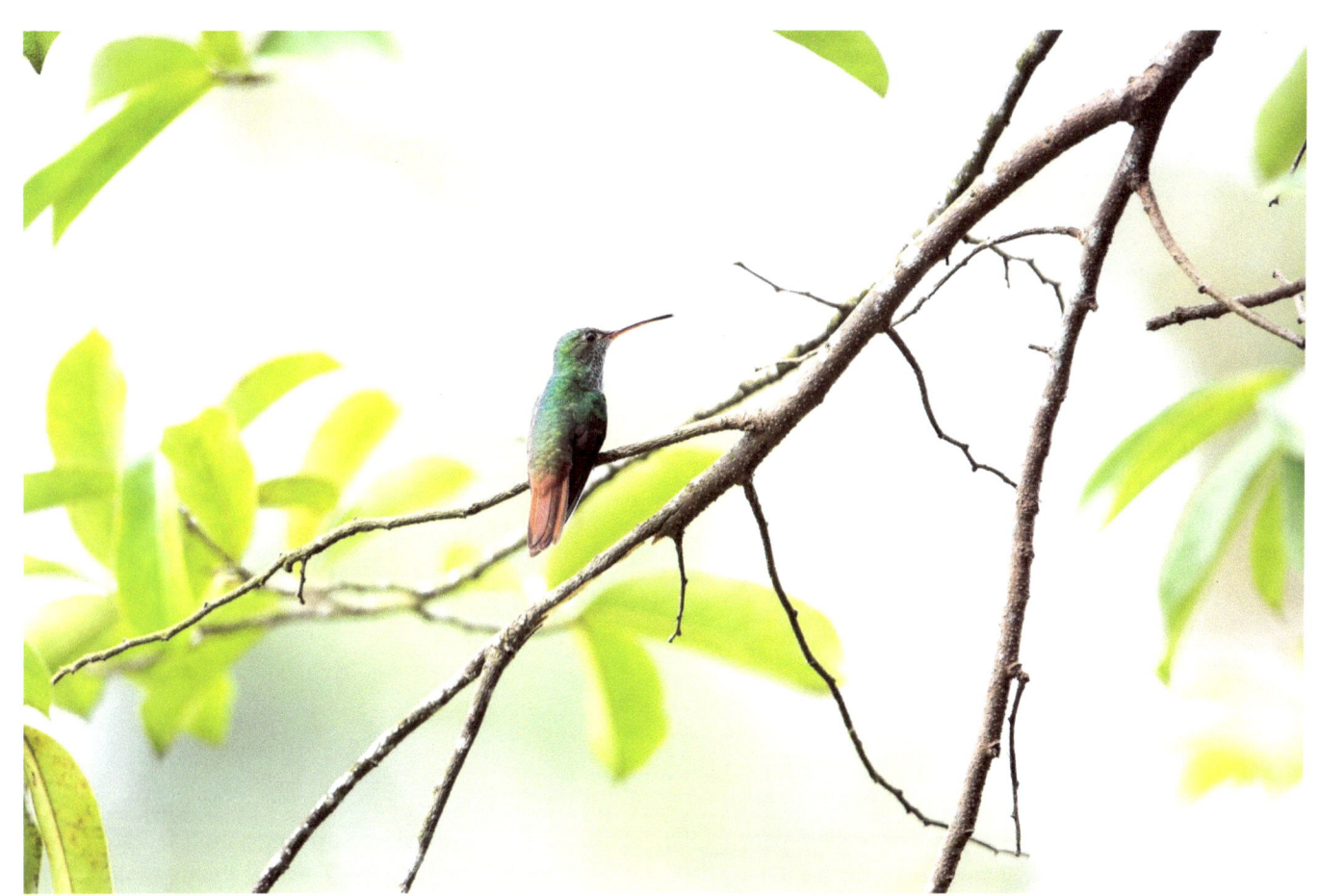

About the Photographers

Amber G. Elliott

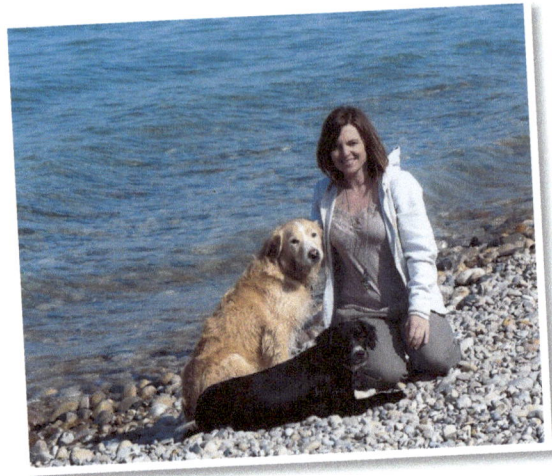

I love Nature. Nature is one of my biggest inspirations. To share my unique vision of the natural world with others is one of my passions. I strive to identify beauty in the smallest of details and to combine the drama of nature with the art of creative media. Growing up in Northern Michigan, I was greatly influenced by the beauty and serenity of the Great Lakes region, and this helped define my future path.

Early in life, I became interested in wildlife conservation and sought to bring light to many causes with an emphasis in preserving wild horses throughout the US. I rescued more animals than I can count before I was 10 and realized at a very young age that I had an intuitive connection with animals.

I began riding horses at age 5, learning dog obedience training through 4-H when I was 8 yrs old and training horses through Natural Horsemanship at age 13. My current four-legged best friend is Cody, a stray dog who found ME and since has never left my side.

The steady presence of animals in my life has shaped who I am today and I proudly serve as a Board Member at a non-profit animal welfare organization in my community.

I began my exploration into the right side of my brain at age 27 when I attended Fine Art school. My degree in website design evolved into owning a multifaceted creative media business, Grand Traverse Photography and Design, which incorporates photography, graphic design and video. I have had the blessing of working with clients like HGTV and the Travel Channel, and with local production companies Brauer Productions and Treefort Collective on feature and short films.

My recent trip to Costa Rica to document the native wildlife was one I will always remember. Enjoying the good company of my travel companion, Kimberli, seeing wild animals I had not known existed on this spectacular planet and learning about the amazing conservation efforts of the good people of Costa Rica made it the trip of a lifetime; Pura Vida!

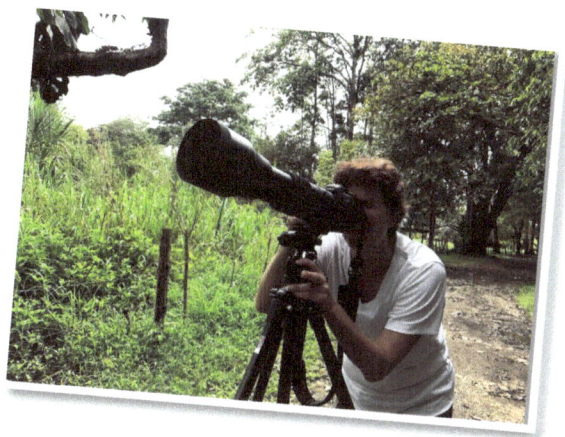

Kimberli A. Bindschatel

Born and raised in Michigan, I spent summers at the lake, swimming, catching frogs, and chasing fireflies, winters building things out of cardboard and construction paper, writing stories, and dreaming of faraway places. Since I didn't make honors English in high school, I thought I couldn't write. So I started hanging out in the art room. The day I borrowed a camera, my love affair with photography began. Long before the birth of the pixel, I was exposing real silver halides to light and marveling at the magic of an image appearing on paper under a red light.

After college, I freelanced in commercial photography studios. During the long days of rigging strobes, stories skipped through my mind. As happens in life though, I was possessed by another dream—to be a wildlife photographer. I trekked through the woods to find loons, grizzly bears, whales, and moose. Then, for six years, I put my heart and soul into publishing a nature magazine, *Whisper in the Woods*. But it was not meant to be my magnum opus. This time, my attention was drawn skyward. I'd always been fascinated by the aurora borealis, shimmering in the night sky, but now my focus went beyond, to the cosmos, to wonder about our place in the universe.

In the spring of 2010, I sat down at the computer, started typing words, and breathed life into a curious boy named Kiran in *The Path to the Sun*. Together, in our quest for truth, Kiran and I have explored the mind and spirit. Our journey has taken us to places of new perspective. Alas, the answers always seem just beyond our grasp, as elusive as a firefly on a warm autumn night.

Most recently, my focus has shifted to more pressing issues—imperiled wildlife. With the Poppy McVie series, I hope to bring some light into the shadowy underworld of black market wildlife trade, where millions of wild animals are captured or slaughtered annually to fund organized crime.

IT. MUST. STOP.

If you'd like to learn more and stay in touch, please sign up for my newsletter or follow my blog at www.KimberliBindschatel.com

www.ingramcontent.com/pod-product-compliance
Lightning Source LLC
Chambersburg PA
CBHW050757180526
45159CB00003B/1496